OFFCUTS 3:
More Stories and Sketches from The Shed

OXLEY MEN'S SHED

OFFCUTS 3:
More Stories and Sketches from The Shed

OXLEY MEN'S SHED

Writers:

Bill Thirkill
William Barker
Jeff Thorpe
Trevor Armstrong
John Brown
Dave Shearer

Graham Trimble
Darryl Dymock
(Editor)
David Hands
Jim Pascoe
James Vernon

Artists:

Peter Darmody
Anthony Durrington
George Pugh

Brian Goeldner
Graham Murphy
Paul Watkins

Offcuts 3: More Stories and Sketches from The Shed

Oxley Men's Shed

© Individual contributors 2024

Published by Armour Books
P. O. Box 492, Corinda QLD 4075

Interior Design and Typeset by Beckon Creative

Cover Image: Original artwork by Peter Darmody

ISBN: 978-1-925380-781

 A catalogue record for this book is available from the National Library of Australia

All rights reserved. No part of this publication may be reproduced, stored in, or introduced into a retrieval system, or transmitted, in any form, or by any means (electronic, mechanical, photocopying, recording or otherwise) without the prior written permission of the publisher.

Note: Australian spelling and grammar conventions are used throughout this book.

Introduction

A Men's Shed is more than the sum of its individual members. Our brochure proclaims that the Oxley Men's Shed provides 'an opportunity for men to work with timber and metal, to write and to draw/paint and connect through group outings. It also provides a space for men to come together and talk, creating all-important social connections and relationships at a vital stage of life.'

The Writers Group is in itself an example of the creativity and camaraderie the *Shed* fosters. We meet fortnightly to share stories and poems from our lives—work experiences, holidays and travels, adventures, family moments, humorous and sometimes dramatic happenings. These are stories that mostly remind us of where we've been on life's journey and of who we are and what we've achieved.

We listen to each other's stories with respect and good humour, and we try to write them better because we want them to make an impact. We're thankful to the President and other Shed members for their encouragement and for regularly giving us a wider audience. For some of us, our families are also a key motivating factor.

The *Offcuts* series continues to provide an important outlet for our writing, and we are grateful to Armour Books for their ongoing support. We've welcomed new writers since the last edition, and their voices add even further to the amazing array of stories and poems included in this volume. We're also delighted to include a few stories from the late Bill Thirkill, who was one of our staunchest members.

Halfway through the year, professional editor Ian Mathieson generously gave us valuable feedback on a selection of the stories we had drafted for *Offcuts 3*. He commented encouragingly that he could see a marked leap in quality from those he'd read a few years back.

Offcuts 3 also benefits once again from contributions by the Shed's talented Art Group. I'm very grateful for the efforts of the gifted Peter Darmody, ably assisted by Anthony Durrington, in creating and collating the drawings and paintings that further bring to life the stories we tell. Unless otherwise shown, the photos in the book were provided by the particular authors.

Readers of the two earlier *Offcuts* books have told us they tend not to read all the stories in one sitting, but dip into them to find those that strike a special chord. I've no doubt that among the 28 stories and poems in *Offcuts 3*, you'll not only discover some fascinating perspectives from the eleven writers represented in this issue, but you'll find a few gems that will add a sparkle to your day.

I wish you Good Reading!

Darryl Dymock
Convenor, Oxley Men's Shed Writers Group
Editor, *Offcuts 3*

Contents

Introduction	v
Bill Thirkill	1
A LOOSE SCREW SAVED TWO LIVES	1
BEING A SOLDIER	3
A FLOODED ROAD, A BROKEN SPRING, A LEAKING RADIATOR — IRAN, 1964	6
William Barker	11
'SAVED' BY THE LOST PATROL	11
THE SANDS OF TIME	18
Jeff Thorpe	25
THE SAD TALE OF *SS TARARUA*	25
Trevor Armstrong	31
TEACHERS I HAVE MOST ADMIRED	31
HERNIA SURGERY AND OTHER PROCEDURES	34
CARING FOR THE ENVIRONMENT	37
Darryl Dymock	43
BEACH HOUSE, BBQS AND BURGERS	43
THEY DO NOT KNOW	50
WHAT DO YOU SAY TO A LIVING GODDESS?	52
Jeff Thorpe	57
HEADING WEST	57
John Brown	63
JOHN AND THE RAINBOW PRINCESS	63

Dave Shearer	77
HOLIDAY ADVENTURES ON THE COORONG, SOUTH AUSTRALIA	77
ROCK AND ROLL	79
Jeff Thorpe	83
THE KOOLAMA AFFAIR	83
Graham Trimble	87
GROWING UP — REAL FAST	87
David Hands	101
THE TEA TREE SCHOOL — A LESSON LEARNT	101
GOING TROPPO IN TONGA	106
Jeff Thorpe	115
TEA OR COFFEE?	115
Jim Pascoe	119
A NIGHT AT THE OPERA	119
THE HOLIDAY THAT WASN'T	122
WHO'S COUNTING?	128
James Vernon	135
FORE!	135
MAZEPA RIDES AGAIN	140
GUN SHY	144
Jeff Thorpe	151
DISASTER ON THE DERWENT	151
The Writers	157
The Artists	

Bill Thirkill

A LOOSE SCREW SAVED TWO LIVES

AS A PLUMBER, I WAS CALLED on for many aspects of the trade as well as some things a little out of my usual line of work. One day I had an urgent request to repair a roof leak, as water had been dripping into an office of Roma Street Railway Station, doing damage.

I arrived at the site and was shown the problem. On inspection I could see that the leak was from a Super Six fibro roof which was very steep. The rain had stopped the previous day but there were heavy, foreboding clouds. The office people were very worried and hoped there might be time to fix the leak before more rain came.

I was told to reach the roof by placing the ladder on the railway line, lean it onto the fibro gutter, climb onto the roof, and have a staff member remove the ladder for trains to come into the station. I was to call out when I was ready to come down. Strangely, I didn't like this idea so looked for another way.

The roof was attached to a brick wall about 20 metres up and, on inspection, I found a window about a metre above where the roof joined the brick wall and about 10 metres to one side. So I decided to climb out the

Peter Darmody

window onto the roof with my tools and repair gear in a bag, make my way to the area where the leak was from, repair it and head back to the window.

I was aware how slippery a fibro roof gets when it's wet, and decided to hurry off it at the first drop of rain.

So, out the window and onto the roof. I located the fault and was repairing it when the first drop arrived. I grabbed my bag and headed for the window.

Too late!

I slipped over onto my bottom and started sliding down the roof, getting faster and faster. I looked down to where I was heading and could see that the only thing to stop me crashing onto the train line was the gutter. However, as it was fibro, I knew it would break easily, and then I would be on the train line.

Well, it got worse. A train was coming. I was going to get run over. I had no chance.

George Pugh

Then a big surprise—the pocket of my shorts hooked itself onto a large sharp washer that was part of a loose screw holding the roof.

That stopped me as I reached the gutter at the same time as the train. *Saved!*

But I was still stuck on the roof, so I climbed onto the roof of the stationary carriage and down the side onto the platform. I walked along in quite a bit of a daze and shaking. *I should be under that train,* I thought.

My repair worked, but even if it hadn't, I wasn't getting back on that roof!

My life was saved by that loose screw, and so was my daughter's life—she was born two years later.

BEING A SOLDIER

My work in the 1950s was as an apprentice plumber with Queensland Rail. As I was soon to turn 18, I received a letter telling me I was required to present myself for Army service for compulsory three months training. But first a medical—all good, and I waited to be taken to the Army training site at Wacol. Suddenly it all came to a halt when National Service was stopped. Instead, I was asked to present myself to an Army Reserve unit.

I joined an anti-tank unit. They taught me how to fire guns and drive strange vehicles called APCs (armoured personnel carriers), plus trucks with crash gearboxes. I really loved these trucks—my favourites were a GMC and a Studebaker. One of these had done only 28 miles, as it had been stored since the war. They were six-wheel drive, with canvas roofs.

I also drove blitz trucks but got into trouble after a puncture outside Gladstone. It took me quite a while to realise that, on the left side of the truck the wheel studs had left-hand threads, and the right side had right-hand threads! Some were troop carriers; others carried the APCs or tanks. In the troop carriers I had the job of driving with about 30 soldiers on the back, very carefully. Most of the guys couldn't drive these trucks as they couldn't work out the crash gearboxes. I'd learned to drive at 16, using crash boxes.

Peter Darmody

One time I was asked to deliver an ambulance from Moorooka to Enoggera. Well, I was a bit naughty. I thought it was okay to have a bit of fun, so I turned on the flashing lights and siren, and off I went. No red lights for me, and all the cars moved out of the way. I had a ball.

After this they decided I would be better in the Signals Corps, so my lanyard was changed from yellow to blue. My epaulets became Royal Australian Signals, and I had much learning to do. I had to know all about radio equipment, telephones and how to connect to the lines, how to set up a network, the phonetic alphabet, so much to know about. Then I was attached to my previous unit, but this time when they were out bush or at a firing range, I would ride in the Jeep once I had the network established.

One training day they were required to shoot a tank look-alike being towed by a tractor with a long chain. It seemed impossible to miss. The thing is that they weren't shooting bombs from the 106-ers that I had when I was an anti-tank gunner. This time they were shooting rockets which seemed to know their job, as they went straight to the target. But if you were behind the launcher you would be just as dead, because a great flame came out as the projectile took off.

They were pleased with the result, as everyone had had a shoot and there were no misses. Then someone said, 'The sig has not had a go, so to make it 100% he should have a shot.'

I looked through the sight, which had been preset, with everyone waiting. Then I noticed a large ironbark tree a little west of the target, but further away. I couldn't resist it, so lined it up, and *bang!* The tree was hit very close to the ground. It blew up and went way up in the air, turned over and came crashing to the ground.

Everyone was looking with absolute amazement on their faces. Then someone said, 'He missed.'

I didn't, of course, but all agreed it was the most spectacular shot all day. And everyone knew I had been pretty naughty.

George Pugh

I did enjoy my Army years, and my work paid my wages whenever I was away, in addition to my Army pay. When the Vietnam war began in the early 1960s, the Army decided they didn't need me, so I headed off to France, and new adventures.

Offcuts 3

A FLOODED ROAD, A BROKEN SPRING, A LEAKING RADIATOR – IRAN, 1964

In 1964 I was leading a coach tour in the Middle East, and drove the tour bus into Iran (previously Persia) via Turkey, passing close to Mount Ararat. This drive was mainly in mountainous country, and the road went through beautiful villages set under steep mountains. The children all looked so nice with their school uniforms and carry-bags. The roads were mostly red dirt and muddy. We drove over 500 kilometres in rain so there was mud over the entire bus. It was so dark inside I could hardly see my passengers, but outside the countryside was beautifully green.

As our two buses arrived at the Iran border the rain stopped, and we proceeded through customs and drove on. However, the waters from the earlier rain had washed away the bridge over the river. A detour would be over 200 kilometres, and we would lose at least a day. It was really cold and the water was rushing down, but I decided to test the depth.

So in my undies I waded across, finding the shallowest part. I had the passengers climb over the remains of the bridge, then drove into the water. But I got stuck, and the men on my bus all stripped down and pushed the bus until I got traction and made it to the other side. The motor and exhaust were very hot and, in no time, I couldn't see the bus for steam. I also had another bus but the driver refused to drive through the water, so I had to do it again. It was better this time, as I knew the track and the boys were pushing.

We drove on east and the road got worse, quite deep corrugations in real desert. Then we came across our first camel train. My passengers were really excited and one young guy had a ride on a camel. When we reached our first town, this was the real Persia, with a loud call to prayer five times a day and other announcements from time to time. There was a lot of interest in our buses, mainly in the women and the kangaroos on each side. I had copied the kangaroos from a penny which I'd traced and expanded. The locals were really friendly, and at cafés many of them came and shook our hands.

George Pugh

We kept breaking springs in the seats. Then the step for getting out of the bus broke. But worse, I broke a spring at the front left axle, and now with the deep ruts the front of the bus would touch the ground. I had to do something, but what? Well, the ladies were reading books and some were finished, so I jacked up the front quite high and fitted the books between each coil, tied them in and lowered the bus. Great—the bus no longer touched the ground. But the road was rough and we broke more seat springs.

Eventually we arrived in Tehran and I could look for someone to replace my spring. But having found someone was only the beginning; explaining the problem was no good until I got him to take a look. Then with a big smile he told me the problem: I had books in my springs. 'No,' I said, 'that was the solution.'

After repairs, I stocked up on supplies and we headed east towards the Afghan border, more terrible roads and dust, but interesting little towns and really friendly people. Sometimes we saw watermelons growing wild in the desert, sometimes there were little streams. Then I noticed the engine was hot and the radiator was leaking. Big problem, especially as we were using up our drinking water. I opened our pepper containers and poured three containers of pepper in and topped up the water, and it worked. The leak stopped and we carried on until I saw a sign for a town we had been told to avoid, but it was the last town before Afghanistan. The temperatures were normally over 40°C there, so it was important to have a good radiator.

Peter Darmody

The town was built around a large mosque so the streets were in circles, and thousands of men were wandering around, a very Shiite Muslim area. I found a radiator repair guy, and he told me to take it out and he would fix it. I told all the women to stay in the bus and keep it locked, but the local men gathered around, staring through the windows at them. It was quite scary.

The repair was done and paid for, and I fitted the radiator. However, I couldn't get the bus out as there were hundreds of men crowded around to look at these western women. So I asked the police to move them, but they had to get the firemen to hose them so I could gradually back the bus out and off.

As I left the town I noticed a British consul's office, and called in to say, 'Good day.' They were delighted to see us, especially to chat up the women. They asked if we had been into the town itself. It seems the last western women in that town had been stoned to death. *Wow!* I could have lost them. We soon waved goodbye and headed into Afghanistan.

That was some 60 years ago. There were lots of challenges in my years of driving buses across more than fifty countries in Europe, Asia and Africa, but also lots of adventures and plenty of fun.

William Barker

'SAVED' BY THE LOST PATROL

NEVER IN MY WILDEST DREAMS would I have thought that I would be sent out as an infantryman on a fighting recon patrol.

As a member of the Royal Australian Army Service Corps, a supporting unit within the Royal Australian Army, my training to fight had been limited to basic training at Kapooka and two weeks at Canungra Jungle Training Centre.

At Nui Dat, I was assigned to the Bulk Store of Australian Army Canteen Unit (ASCU), a non-combatant support unit. The ASCU comprised a PX gift shop, a 1960s version of a JB Hi-Fi, selling everything at tax-free prices. The Bulk Store was a Coles/Woolworths look-alike distribution centre, stocked with everything a small town would consume: from beer, wine and spirits to tinned and packaged food, snacks and toiletries.

Bulk Store and PX Gift Shop in foreground; Luscombe Field – Nui Dat airfield; Long Hai mountains – a Viet Cong stronghold

All the commodities were tax free. For example, a 12-year-old 40oz Chivas Regal whisky sold for $1.20 and a packet of cigarettes was also $1.20.

Offcuts 3

Mine was a relatively safe role, within the limits of the Nui Dat Task Force Base. However, my notion of staying safe was to be seriously challenged after four months in Vietnam.

In August 1969, Tony Stefanou, from the PX section of ASCU, was ordered to be on the first patrol comprising members of the Task Force Maintenance Area (TFMA), the area of Nui Dat that accommodated 12 or more small supporting units of four to eight soldiers—payroll, fuel, post office, signal squadron, field hygiene, ordnance field park, topographical survey troop and many more accommodated within the TFMA tent lines.

Within the Nui Dat Task Force area, three battle-ready battalions ably undertook the reconnaissance and patrol more safely than any members of the Task Force Maintenance Area could. A TFMA patrol would comprise soldiers from supporting units led by equally unqualified officers and non-commissioned officers.

I thought that with Stefanou chosen for the first patrol, my chances of being selected in the near future seemed unlikely. Each afternoon, the TFMA canteen was a gathering point for a chat and a pre-dinner drink. At this time, the conversation centred on the possibility of being chosen in the next batch of TFMA members to do a patrol. The second patrol was already undergoing its ten afternoons' training sessions. A third group was to be ordered to undergo training within the next week.

Scuttlebutt and furphies circulated freely during the drinking times at the canteen as we consumed our allocated two cans of beer per man per day. The gossip was fascinating and diverse.

One rumour received most attention. The TFMA commanding officer was said to be a frustrated infantry officer, trying to 'big note' himself and gain some military honours. He was considered to be the instigator of the patrol idea and to have put the idea to the Task Force commander as a way to take some pressure off the battalions and to give him some infantry credence.

On Saturday 9 August 1969, my complacency was to be dramatically shattered. The day began like any other day in Vietnam: awoke, shaved, dressed, breakfasted and at work from 08:00 hours. The walk to work each morning was through the rubber plantation, under which our sandbagged tents were situated, past the cook house and mess hall, and along the sloping path between the sergeants' lines and the security fence around the Bulk Store—a walk I had done countless times since arriving at Nui Dat. The last part was to walk behind the PX and its storage shed.

As I went past Lieutenant Ward's ASCU office at the rear of the PX to enter through the gates of the Bulk Store, he called out to me. (Lieutenant Ward was a baby-faced National Serviceman, a couple of years younger than myself. He did the National Servicemen's officers' course—the short course—at Scheyville, Victoria.)

As I stood at ease in front of his desk, Lieutenant Ward began: 'Private Barker, you know that Private Tony Stefanou is out on patrol with the force comprised of TFMA personal. He's on a reconnaissance fighting patrol. Another group from the TFMA is now doing its ten afternoons' training sessions ready to be deployed as soon as the first patrol returns.'

I stood silent, maintaining eye contact with the lieutenant as he continued. 'On the Monday 18 August 1969 at 1500 hours, you are required to report to the Task Force Headquarters to commence your ten afternoon training sessions as a member of the third patrol from TFMA. You will be ready to take over from the second patrol.'

Softening the directive, Lieutenant Ward continued: 'I find you reliable, trustworthy and considerate of your mates. I believe that you would stick by them through thick and thin. You would be a good soldier to have on patrol. Any questions?'

George Pugh

'Yes, sir, who is leading the patrol?'

'The sergeant from the TFMA Q-Store.'

My reaction was explosive. 'He's a bloody idiot. He couldn't lead a patrol through the Q-Store let alone out in the bush.'

My initial contact with the sergeant had been when I was issued with my kit on arrival at Nui Dat. I was not impressed with our first meeting. Lieutenant Ward, startled by my spontaneous reaction, just sat there and stared at me.

I continued: 'Sir, are you ordering me at this time?'

'No, the order will come later in the week.'

Monday morning 11 August began a very different week. We started with the Bulk Store closed for the day while the blue Military Payment Certificate (MPC), the currency for the Allied forces in Vietnam used on all military alliance bases, was collected and replaced with a new red MPC. On Tuesday the blue MPC would not be acceptable as currency.

On Wednesday Captain Tue, commander of the Vietnamese forces in the Vung Tau area of Phuc Tuy Province, a regular visitor, arrived with the new red MPC. Where he'd obtained it, we did not ask. Whenever he came, he was accompanied by his personal barber. We all had our hair cut at no cost to us. I knew that I would look good on patrol.

On Thursday morning, as I passed Lieutenant Ward outside the PX, I asked: 'Sir, are you still ordering me to attend patrol training?'

'No, that will come tomorrow.'

The different week continued. Unknown to all of us privates in the Bulk Store and including our Warrant Officer, Eric Matherson, we'd been given a reinforcement, Jeff, to add to the Bulk Store staff. WO Matherson became annoyed at the lack of information and communication, and stormed off to confront Lieutenant Ward. It was fascinating to stand on the sidelines and watch their interaction.

The week's distractions kept my mind off what could happen while out on patrol and, especially, how I would react if we came under enemy fire. This was a complete unknown. I did not have the experience of the war games that the infantry plays during its training.

The order for me to report to Task Force Headquarters was finally given on Friday morning. Wardie was casually waiting for me to come down to work, SLR in hand, with the three other blokes from our tent.

'Private Barker, a moment please. I am ordering you to report to Task Force Headquarters on Monday at 1500 hours to commence your patrol training.'

That was that. There were no more games I could have played beyond disobeying the order and being charged. I had to do the training and to go out on patrol.

Peter Darmody

I went to church on Sunday, as I had done as frequently as I was able to since arriving in Vietnam. They were quick and to-the-point services.

Monday 18 August came all too quickly. Work was normal: packing orders, driving my little Ferguson forklift, unloading trucks and taking a full hour for lunch.

At 1430 hours, I reported to Lieutenant Ward's office. He gave me the ASCU's Land Rover to drive to Task Force Headquarters on the other side of Nui Dat hill. I drove slowly so as not to be too early.

As I approached the headquarters, a plain, long galvanised low-set metal building with many louvered windows set on a concrete slab, the only distinguishing feature was the sign, *Restricted area, Keep out*. There seemed to be no abnormal activity. No troops standing around, waiting for orders. *Maybe they are somewhere out of sight waiting*, I thought.

I entered the office and presented myself to the duty sergeant sitting behind a large wooden desk, telling him who I was and why I was there.

He looked at me questioningly. He went on: 'Private Barker, you should've been told that the services of the TFMA personnel are no longer required for patrol duties. The present patrol became lost and disorientated in a forest of bamboo. A search was mounted by Iroquois helicopters, much needed in support of the battalion's current operations.[1] Some members of the patrol were dehydrated. The whole exercise resulted in unnecessary time expended to find and then extract them from the area back to Nui Dat.'

He finished with the wonderful words: 'Your services are no longer required.'

With a smile and an unfettered sense of relief, I thanked the sergeant and turned towards the door. The weight of the last couple of weeks had lifted; and with a sense of gratitude and concern for the lost patrol members, I returned to the Land Rover.

Anthony Durrington

---

1   *Operation Camden*, 9 July to 30 Aug 1969. The Australian Army 5th Battalion, Royal Australian Regiment was supporting the 501 Land Clearing Company, United States Army Corps of Engineers which was undertaking land-clearing operations in the Hat Dich area. Source: Lieutenant-Colonel Fred Fairhead, *A Duty Done*, The Royal Australian Regiment Association, pp. 98–101.

The lost patrol's predicament had highlighted the lack of training of TFMA personnel and why they should not be used for reconnaissance patrols. Their misfortune was my good luck. I would never know how I might have reacted, had I come under enemy fire.

Driving hastily, but keeping to the speed limit, I returned the Land Rover to the Bulk Store compound, with a feeling of satisfaction. I had quietly protested to Lieutenant Ward and was a little thankful that the lost patrol had come into difficulty when it did it and so altered the thinking of the Headquarters command.

The patrol returned with only minor injuries and dehydration; and its personnel went back to their various work stations, after a few days rest and recuperation (R&R) in Vung Tau.

I had a few beers with the boys while telling them the good news.

THE SANDS OF TIME

A warm, early spring day in 1970 was a good day to be active. I was home safe from Vietnam and enjoying my freedom.

My mother, Britha, had taken my young brothers to school and came to check if I needed anything done at the shop we had leased.

After returning from Vietnam in mid-May 1970 and being recently discharged from National Service, I had a substantial amount of savings. There had been little to buy in Vietnam.

I had applied for and had been accepted in mature-age enrolment at the University of Queensland. As an interim measure and a job, I had entered into a partnership with my parents in a mixed business on the Gold Coast Highway at Mermaid Beach. We had bought the lease. The business was run down, but had potential. Having been 2IC of the Bulk Store at Nui Dat had given me the confidence to take over the lease. It was an important step before I commenced studies at the University of Queensland in March 1971.

My parents' concern about my future on my return from Vietnam was based on their memories of returning soldiers from World War Two. Their idea of my running the business was their way to help me settle back into civilian life after two years in the army, with one year in Vietnam.

Running a grocery store was not an entirely different or new family venture. My parents had been business pioneers in the outer rural Brisbane suburb of Kenmore where, in the 1950s, they built and ran a mixed business and opened the first post office at Kenmore, at the time known as Kenmore Junction. The grocery shop and post office were located on Moggill Road across from

Barker's mixed business and Post Office, with chemist on the left and doctor's surgery on the right; Moggill Rd, Kenmore, 1950s.

the Kenmore State School, a one-teacher school in the 1950s, run by Mr. Smethurst. Later, the block of shops was extended to accommodate a pharmacy and a doctor's surgery.

An ever-growing family of eight sons and a daughter was the compelling force behind the venture, enabling my parents to feed, clothe and educate us. In the years to come, the family grew to 10 sons and a daughter.

My father, Noel, did not give up his position in the Standard Insurance Company in Eagle Street, Brisbane City. So, out of school time, it was essential for the older three boys, Anthony, Brian and myself to assist. We would serve customers in the shop and post office as well as pricing goods and stocking shelves.

On one occasion, Brian and I caught a bus to travel to Shearer's Bakery in Taringa to collect fresh bread. We missed the returning connection. There was not another bus until late in the afternoon. We walked the 3.8 miles (6.1 km) to the Kenmore shop, each carrying a sugar bag of high-top bread.

Telegrams also needed to be delivered. We walked or rode our only bike—a full-sized men's bike donated by our uncle John—along the many dirt side-roads, delivering telegrams.

The Mermaid Beach store was located in a block of other businesses on the western side of the Pacific Highway. Each morning at 6, I would open the doors and set up for the day's trading, making sure the shop was clean and tidy. Fresh milk and bread would arrive at an early hour and had to be put away ready for sale. New stock was marked and put on the shelves, and fridges re-organised for the long day's trading, seven days a week.

Mum would come in later each morning after she had dropped my young brothers at school. She would stay until the end of school time. I kept the shop open until 9 pm.

Barker's mixed business, 2440 Gold Coast Highway, Mermaid Beach, 1970.

On an inviting, warm, sunny spring morning, I asked Mum if she would look after the shop while I had a quick surf. She said yes; so off I went.

As I looked down from the sand hills, I saw the local council-funded lifesaver was on duty a little way along the beach towards Surfers Paradise. The flags were up. Life was worth living. I was Army-fit and suntanned and wearing new speedos. I looked the part. The surf was inviting, with smooth, rolling white-capped waves. I dropped my towel and shirt on the golden sand. In I went.

Offcuts 3

On my left wrist was my waterproof-to-30-metres stainless-steel, automatic self-winding Seiko watch that I had purchased in Vietnam for $20. I could wear it anywhere, so the instruction booklet said. The watch was perfect for the surf, and I would be able to keep track of the time. I did not want to be away from the shop for too long.

The waves were perfect for body-surfing; large, rounding with an even curl, taking me for a long ride right into the shallow water. I kept pace with the waves. I was enjoying the freedom of being away from the shop and the independence from the regimentation of the Army and the Vietnam war.

After surfing many waves into the beach, I glanced at my left wrist to check the time, knowing I should return to the shop and let Mum go and do other things. But to my utter surprise, my watch had vanished. It was no longer on my wrist. My waterproof-to-30 metres stainless-steel, automatic self-winding Seiko watch had vanished beneath the waves into the sands of Mermaid Beach.

Desperately, I searched by diving under the waves and running my hands through the sand to no avail, a fruitless search. It wasn't long before I came to an abrupt conclusion. I had no hope of finding the watch. I had lost it in the salty golden sands of Mermaid Beach; a precious memento of my time in Vietnam.

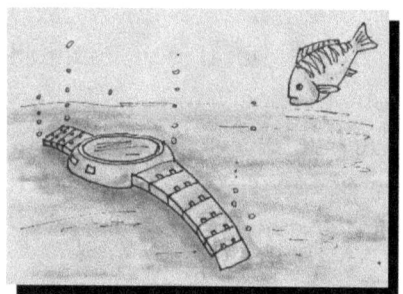

Anthony Durrington

I could do nothing more. I was dejected yet consoled as I still had a gold Seiko dress watch which I had also bought in Vietnam. Saddened by the loss of a memento from my time in that country, I returned to the shop and continued working, as I had been doing over the previous couple of months.

Late in the morning the next day, Mum sent me off for a break. With the disappointment from the loss still lingering, I decided to go for another surf to freshen up. I walked across the highway and down Venice Street to the beach. As I stood on the sand hill overlooking the beach, I glanced to my left. The flags were flying. Further along was Surfers Paradise. I was a little later than the day before. The tide was in at about the same height.

I paused and reflected on the previous day's loss and stared into the waves. *Out there in the sand beneath the waves was my Seiko watch, gone forever.* Dispirited by the loss, I walked to the flagged area, put my towel on the sand and waded into the surf.

I was in no hurry. I was waist deep. As I was about to dive under the incoming wave, I stood on something unusual, something hard buried in the soft sand. Curious to know what it was, I braced myself against the next wave and, as I carefully lifted my foot, I bent down with both hands cupped and grabbed at the sand.

To my absolute amazement, there, in my sand-covered hands, was my waterproof-to-30 metres

Peter Darmody

Offcuts 3

stainless-steel, automatic self-winding Seiko watch, ticking happily away. Beyond expectation.

I was overjoyed. I immediately ended any thought of my surfing for the day.

Every day since the miraculous find, I have worn my waterproof-to-30 meters, stainless-steel, automatic self-winding Seiko watch, EXCEPT WHEN I GO SWIMMING.

JEFF THORPE

THE SAD TALE OF THE *SS TARARUA*

SHIP BUILDERS MUST SWELL with pride when one of theirs meets fame,
and mourn if disaster strikes a craft that bears their name.
Such would be the case for Gourlay Brothers of Dundee
with *Tararua's* sinking in an unforgiving sea.
A screw-driven steamship built in eighteen sixty-four,
one of 230 that hailed from Gourlay's door,
owned by Union Steamship Co, three-masted and twin-engined
she made New Zealand history, though surely not intentioned.

On 29 April 1881, *Tararua* sailed from Port Chalmers bound for Bluff,
then continue on to Melbourne, a course known well enough,
a regular passenger service with one-fifty-one aboard,
Melbourne arrival that one officer looked toward.
Ship's Captain Frank Garrard was travelling to his wedding,
little knowing the tragedy to which his ship was heading.
Near dawn on the next morning the ship struck Otara Reef
off Waipapa Point, the start of unimaginable grief.

Offcuts 3

Rocks broke the vessel's propeller and unshipped its rudder,
pinning it to the reef with an unrelenting shudder.
The first lifeboat holed on launching, a second reached the land,
though with sparse population, no help was at hand.
A telegraph was sent to Dunedin asking for support,
ironically not marked urgent, thus assistance fell well short.
By noon the wind had risen and the swell intensified,
another lifeboat capsized, seven would-be swimmers died.

Wreck of SS Tamarua: *Illustrated New Zealand Herald*, Dunedin. Public domain.

The ship was breaking up, and first the stern went under,
passengers clinging to wreckage quickly dashed asunder,
The only lifeboat left could not breach the waves,
numerous poor souls were dispatched to watery graves.
Those left on board moved forward, clinging to the rigging,
but regrettably their fate was sealed, the elements
    unremitting.
2:30 next morning were heard the last victims' cries,
at daybreak only floating wreckage—the sea had claimed its
    prize.

To this day New Zealand's worst civilian shipping disaster,
one hundred and thirty-one passed on to their hereafter,
only twenty persons survived, for days bodies swept ashore,
a graveyard set up at Otara, on land vacant before.
Known as Tararua Acre, fifty-five were buried there,
and a plaque erected to commemorate the sad affair.
Initially Captain Garrard was interred at this ground,
but later reburied at Christchurch in a pioneer compound.

A Court of Inquiry assigned much blame to Captain Garrard
plus lookout Seaman Weston, for failing to safeguard
Tararua's position, which was too close to the shoreline
and could have been rectified by use of a lead line.
Some say Garrard a scapegoat with no right of reply,
though with such a great catastrophe, facts awkward to
    deny,
yet two important recommendations came from the Inquiry,
vital for future shipping and having no expiry.

OFFCUTS 3

Firstly, the need for a lighthouse at Waipapa Point,
an endorsement that for mariners did not disappoint.
Tararua not alone in perishing at Waipapa,
Otara Reef for shipping a major handicapper:
the barque *William Ackers* wrecked there five years before,
eight of eleven crew the greatest sacrifice bore.
As such, in 1884 a lighthouse built and lit,
for nine nautical miles does the powerful beam emit.

The second recommendation dealt with lifebelt provision,
for maritime safety, a no-brainer decision.
Incredibly, *Tararua* had only twelve lifebelts on board,
woefully inadequate and not to be ignored.
Not unexpected, the Court forthwith instituted
lifebelts for all passengers and crews, an order undisputed.
As well the Inquiry directed, lifeboat drills to be compulsory,
and held at stated intervals, not treated as perfunctory.

Major edicts certainly, yet little consolation
for those whose lives were lost in utter desolation.
A tragedy by all accounts which could have been prevented;
instead, a stain on history that has been long lamented.
A bitter lesson learned to promote safety on the ocean,
achieved it must be said with vast outpouring of emotion.
One-thirty-one reasons why seafarers of today
owe a debt to *Tararua* every time they cast away.

Brian Goeldner

Trevor Armstrong

TEACHERS I HAVE MOST ADMIRED

TEACHERS CAN HAVE a strong influence on us in childhood and often leave lasting impressions on young minds.

My early childhood opportunities did not include pre-school or prep teachers, but my Sunday School Kindergarten experiences included Rosewood Congregational Church parents and their children—'tweens' and teenagers teaching Bible stories through pictures, and colouring-in depictions as teams.

Miss Cannon was our first Grade One teacher, who taught us classmates patiently through painting on sheets clamped to easels and allowed us to take items home to show our families.

Miss Thurlow, I remember, was our freshly trained Grade Two Teacher who patiently taught us our alphabet, to print, read and basic arithmetic.

In March 1957 our dairy farm and milk run were sold to a Victorian family—so our family moved from the 7-Mile on the Bremer River banks, Rosewood, to 24 Brisbane Road, East Ipswich. This large home and surrounding allotments (with an air raid shelter) were formerly owned by the *Scotts of Ipswich*, family manufacturers of steel products.

Offcuts 3

From co-educational Rosewood School with my twin sister and brothers, I was transferred to Ipswich Central Boys' School in Milford Street, Ipswich, and allocated to a Grade 4 Class of around 40 fellow students. It was a much more crowded classroom and school, and the grounds had barely a blade of grass surviving on the sporting fields. There were neighbouring separate Girls', Infants' and Opportunity Schools, plus Claremont Centre for disabled children.

I remember my new teacher printing his name, *Norman Bryce*, 28 Quarry Street, Ipswich, on our class blackboard—an address which I later realised was opposite one of our fresh milk-run customer's family rented home complexes. He was tall with two ambitious older sons, wore long sleeves, trousers and tie, and welcomed us with mutual respect by imparting useful information that we could apply to our developing daily lives.

We made lasting friendships with mates from Aboriginal communities who became fellow monitors for preparing pots of tea for the teachers' lunchroom. We were entrusted with the duties of cleaning, which included washing, drying and lining up cups on the windowsill. One day we knocked a cup off that fell down two storeys on to flat bitumen below without breaking. It was noted by our Headmaster, *Mr Black*, who immediately brought it up to the lunchroom. He later threatened our class

Peter Darmody

by bending the cane, which broke unexpectedly in his hands—causing him to embarrassingly place the smaller end of the cane into our bin.

During interesting science periods, we learnt timely lessons on how Russian and US satellites were launched and rotated around our earth and could be viewed nightly by our families—information that was really appreciated in the late 1950s. Fellow students and our parents welcomed extending this teacher's lead of our class into Grade 5. I later visited him and his wife at their home to thank him for lessons learnt.

Our new Headmaster was *Mr de Jersey*. His son Paul, who much later became Governor of Queensland, was allocated to our class. He graduated after the Year 8 Scholarship examination to the more prestigious Ipswich Boys Grammar School, whereas I preferred to attend the new co-educational Bremer State High School at Silkstone. It had a variety of teachers with practical skills in coaching athletics, and I became involved in State sprinting competitions at the Exhibition ovals, long distance endurance running, and representative rugby league.

We had developed Central Boys Rules football at primary school, but preferred co-ed basketball games at Bremer High School during our enjoyable lunch hour. Our English teacher was *Mr Collins*, who helped Aboriginal families to save up to move from humpies at Churchill/Yamanto to more substantial homes with better prospects and living standards.

Mr Noel Brady was our Deputy Principal at Bremer High and chastised me as a poor School Prefect example for being late to parade, until he realised I'd already ridden my bike to serve multiple milk-run customers on the other side of Ipswich each day. From that time he praised my tenacity as an example to his family and fellow students living nearby.

Thus, these teachers were most admired and helped me learn valuable life lessons that stood with me to persevere at tasks and to understand subjects from primary, secondary and university studies which I have been able to apply to solve everyday practical problems for the betterment of our society.

HERNIA SURGERY AND OTHER PROCEDURES

In early 2021 when I was lifting my motor mower back into my Triton 4WD ute after having it serviced at Corinda Mower Services, I experienced a hernia protrusion from my alimentary canal in my left genital area.

My GP advised me that he had booked me into Princess Alexandra Hospital (PAH) for hernia surgery from April, 2021. However, he said there was no urgency unless the hernia became twisted—then just ring 000 for emergency corrections.

At subsequent GP consultations for new and continuing health issues and prescriptions, I continually told him my hernia was getting worse and causing more problems. So I asked and was assured by the GP that he was renewing his requests for prioritising PAH hernia elective surgery.

Though I usually have a high pain threshold, in April 2024 I experienced increasing pain while operating a soil auger when helping to plant 100 native trees, shrubs and groundcovers for a CreekCare group working bee. I crawled, with my wife Carol's help, up our home stairs to shower and change clothes, then phoned 000.

I lay on our bed until two paramedics arrived in our driveway. They asked plenty of questions, gave me two 500 mg paracetamol tablets for pain relief and stretchered me to their ambulance. They told me PAH was full up with emergencies, so asked if I would agree to be transported to Queen Elizabeth II Hospital (QEII H) at Coopers Plains.

Immediately I agreed as I had previous successful operations there for fractured and crushed T12 vertebrae when I fell from my extension ladder onto a smooth, slippery concrete floor while cleaning out my large farm shed on the Australia Day public holiday in 2019. The cleanout was forced on me when the planned Inland Freight Rail Line from Melbourne Port to Brisbane resumed the last of my 132-acre farm at Mt Forbes Road, Ebenezer, near Ipswich.

My previous QEII H stay was with my wife in July 2021, when we broke our sternums as our Mitsubishi Magna sedan was written off in a head-on collision with a young driver, who immediately admitted he went through a red-light turning arrow.

That was when a paramedic first detected abnormal anti-arrhythmic gaps in my cardiograph, and they kept me in QEII H longer than my wife and daughter wished.

When I was finally processed through Emergency via paramedics at QEII H on Thursday, 11 April 2024 (just two days after my, and my twin sister's, 76th birthday) medical staff encouraged me to try to push my hernia back inside, but without much lasting success.

They promised to arrange for the boss surgeon to operate on my hernia within a month, and I was discharged with a letter after 9:00 pm on the same day. I made my way home via a friendly Congolese immigrant Uber driver.

On Monday 13 May I had an adult health care check of heart referral etc. at Blunder Road Oxley Medical Centre by a care plan nurse, which was free for 75+ year olds, and I was cleared as OK to operate. So, on the mornings of Mondays 20 May and 3 June, my wife joined me for pre-admission for general surgery interviews at QEII H with an anaesthetist, a cardiologist, a pharmacist and other medical staff, which went well.

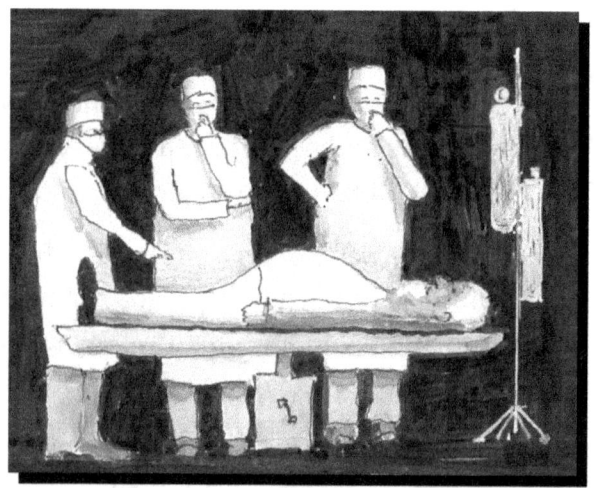

Peter Darmody

Early on Monday 17 June I was transported by a neighbouring BushCare helper to QEII H Day Surgery Reception where I was proficiently prepared for my hernia surgery in a back-to-front blue gown, and kept warmer in the cool air-conditioning to reduce dangerous germs infection, by a warmed blanket.

Between 1 pm and 3 pm, surgery was carried out efficiently after a lower back morphine injection into my spine to keep me awake while young surgeon Dr Julia performed what she said was the largest hernia and screen protection insertion she had performed so far. Recovery room lasted for another two hours. The medical team there, and at bed 22, ward 2B with nurse Lynn, cared for me with paracetamol painkillers throughout that day and night until I was transferred to the transit lounge where I had lunch, more monitoring, and treatments. I was discharged at 4 pm, when my daughter could drive me home.

Follow-up care was by my Care Team nurse, Lynn, who advised me to leave the surgical skin dressings for at least one week after surgery. My positive QEII H experiences led me back to healthy BushCare experiences, but with restricted lifting duties. I was glad to be allowed to drive—even a manual ute—so I could resume efficient environmental links maintenance.

CARING FOR THE ENVIRONMENT

'Congratulations on managing to convert problem weeds infesting Pennywort Creek catchment to safe native habitat corridors!' This is the sort of welcome compliment my fellow BushCarers hear from neighbours as they enjoy walking about our local council parks.

My background in caring for the environment started in the 1950s when I was living on our dairy farm along the Bremer River at 7-Mile Creek crossing, two miles east of Rosewood in south-east Queensland, with my seven siblings, including my twin sister.

OFFCUTS 3

We helped dad and mum prepare, cultivate, plant, irrigate and harvest crops, and to breed, feed and milk dual purpose Red Poll cows—from 3 am and 3 pm every day of the year—through droughts, fires and floods. Daily chores included delivering fresh milk (before refrigeration became commonplace) via tapped cans and measuring billy cans to many appreciative customers in Ipswich before changing our clothes and riding our bikes to school.

After graduating in Agricultural Science from the University of Queensland, I hitch-hiked through Indonesia, Malaysia and Thailand to the 'Golden Triangle' between Laos and Burma to examine Australian Development Aid Abroad's Project—trying to demonstrate growing upland rice instead of opium poppies. At the end of my travels I accepted a Queensland Lands Department agronomist job.

From 1971, I was employed to evaluate the prospect of developing vacant Crown land in wallum coastal lowlands. However, all sizes were uneconomical, so I was seconded to the Western Arid Region Land Use Study of the area known as 'Heartbreak Corner' in south-west Queensland.

I was also called on to study, examine, write and present as an Expert Witness at Land Courts throughout Queensland on a new cattle standard for assessing Crown leasehold rents—until the worldwide crash of cattle prices in 1974.

From 1975 to 2006 I was employed as a Weeds Research Agronomist based in Sherwood's Alan Fletcher Research Station where the Commonwealth Prickly Pear Commission had investigated and established the *Cactoblastis cactorum* moth from Argentina to biologically control this cactus invasion covering 25 million acres and spreading at one million acres per year in 1921.

Our team of entomologists, agronomists, botanists, chemists, plant pathologists, experimentalists and extension officers developed successful programs of Integrated Weeds Management to demonstrate at public events such as Field Days.

During this time, my link with the family farm was renewed when in 1980 I inherited two paddocks in Ebenezer, finishing on the corner of Ebenezer Road and Armstrong Lane, plus land at Mt Forbes Road, a total of 234 acres, to manage cattle breeding. I built a diversion bank to a ten megalitre dam which was designed to never go dry, based on past rainfall records. However, the stored water evaporated during the 1990s droughts.

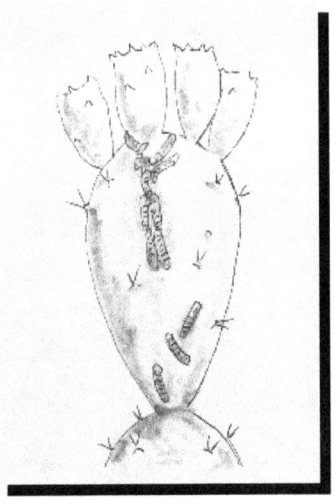

Anthony Durrington

This property was bisected by a high voltage transmission power tower with lines from Swanbank Powerhouse to Toowoomba, plus a large microwave tower on the top of the hill. I built a large shed, new fences and mustering yards nearby.

However, all the land was resumed for the proposed Inland Freight Rail Line, intended to run from Melbourne to Brisbane. I sold my grandfather's original homestead property to my youngest brother's eldest son for his family's horse stud.

Now that I've retired from paid employment, I use the knowledge, skills and experience I've accrued to devote myself to caring for the local environment in the local community. There are many needs, and also good people working together to help meet them.

Offcuts 3

Peter Darmody

BushCare professionals and volunteers continually implement programs to convert weedy infestations progressively into native plant, animal and micro-organisms habitats. (Environmental weeds are any undesirable, non-indigenous plants that are introduced to that diverse native habitat and that compete with the natural environment.)

Aerial photos from the 1930s depict winding Pennywort Creek and its tributaries between Corinda to Oxley Creek slowly distributing water, sediments and flood debris downstream to Moreton Bay. Since Brisbane City Council organised contractors with machinery to straighten banks and clean out channels for 'flood mitigation', faster flows are causing erosion of alluvial soils and washing out associated plants.

Alongside Pennywort Creek, Corinda Golf Course office staff warn golfers not to venture into adjacent bushland if they inadvertently hit their golf ball off the fairway 'as insurance claims do not cover them for snake bite.' When I encounter stray golf balls in 'snake habitat', I throw them back to just inside the verge, to avoid them being mowed. However, golfing males claim they don't reuse second-hand balls as they 'have enough other reasons to blame for bad shots.'

Others, especially women golfers, have no qualms in using recycled balls and rarely encounter troublesome native snakes as the reptiles sense you coming through bushy areas and slide away to safe, sunny sites.

Volunteers are always welcome to join our teams regularly helping control environmental weed infestations to reclaim our native habitat corridors. There are regular 'Prepare to Plant' working bees on environmental weeds sites in local parks. Linking them to recently resumed flooded allotments by BushCare volunteers promises to reclaim biodiverse native habitat corridors for the benefit of whole communities.

Darryl Dymock

BEACH HOUSE, BBQS AND BURGERS

ON THE DAY OF OUR ARRIVAL at *Beach House** we were about 15 minutes away and still hadn't received the check-in code that had been promised for our contactless arrival.

'*On our way,*' I texted. '*Please send code.*'

'*Oh yes,*' came the instant reply, with a smiley face, as if they'd forgotten we were coming. '*Front door is unlocked. Key on bench. We used to leave it under the mat but it seems to be rusting.*' It was signed '*Sally*'. So much for the code we'd been expecting.

This turned out to be the beginning of some interesting text exchanges with Sally.

We followed her loose directions and, after looping around the small town a couple of times, came across a faded sign proclaiming *Beach House*. After negotiating deep muddy ruts that would've swallowed a Fiat 500 without a trace, we pulled up on a patch of thick green grass near the front (or was it the back?) door.

We were at this holiday location because only a few weeks before Christmas our daughter had texted us. '*Cheap fares in January. Do you want to come over?*' She and our two grandkids were on holidays.

Offcuts 3

We flew over for a week. In the meantime, we'd booked this place on the coast for three nights so our son-in-law could come too. A whole house—four bedrooms, more than enough for the six of us, although only one bathroom—part of a bigger apartment complex. At an eye-watering cost because there wasn't much around at short notice.

George Pugh

As we climbed stiff-limbed from the car, towering over us on one side was a faded red shipping container covered in even more faded stickers and symbols. On the other side of us was a rusty framework of iron pipes, groaning under the weight of a motley collection of bleached timber that looked as if it'd been salvaged long ago because it might come in handy someday.

The older-style single-level timber house was painted white throughout and had been re-shaped inside, with walls knocked out and repositioned. I wouldn't go so far as to call it a renovation, however. Although it didn't affect our group, the only access to one bedroom was through another bedroom. There was a mysterious black steel plate inserted in the timber kitchen floor for no apparent purpose and, in the lounge room, the plasterboard ceiling had been patched with a large screwed-on unpainted panel of five-ply timber.

An uncovered side-deck with a wooden table and hard chairs without cushions overlooked a lagoon about 50 metres away, promising kayaking adventures during our stay. The kayaks and vests were part of the deal.

We'd brought sausages for our evening meal, and as the sun started to set I went to check on the barbecue on the deck. There were two of them—one gas, one electric. I took the cover off the gas barbie. The hotplate was covered in a layer of rust so thick I doubt an industrial grinder would have made any impression on it.

The electric barbecue was a George Foreman grill. Its hotplate wasn't rusty, just bearing the baked-on remains of whatever gastronomic delights the last people to use it had enjoyed. What's more, the electric cable was draped across the cooktop, with no sign of a power point.

I'm sure George wouldn't have been pleased, and neither was I. We were paying a lot of money for this place.

'Hi Sally,' I texted. 'Disappointed with state of BBQs. One rusted and unusable, and the George Foreman not cleaned after last use. Can't see power point either. Was expecting better for what we are paying.'

I received a quick reply: 'Oh dear, the last people must've not cleaned it!!'

D'oh. I could see that.

Then another text pinged: 'Electric one you have to feed cord through kitchen window.'

What sort of Mickey Mouse setup is this? I thought.

Annoyed, I replied: 'I thought BBQs would be checked and cleaned if necessary as part of your quality check processes. We are cooking indoors instead.'

Sally: 'Usually people are good. This has been overlooked.'

I suspected that what had been overlooked was any check on facilities other than the usual whip-around by the cleaners between guests.

In my head I started wording the review I was going to post online.

Next morning at breakfast we found in the cupboard three small, patterned bowls that'd be good for noodles, and two large white bowls you might serve spaghetti in. But no cereal-sized bowls. This was in a house intended to sleep up to nine people.

We ate our cereal in shifts—washing and swapping the small bowls.

In my head I added to my online review.

As we contemplated our day, a text arrived from Sally. 'Hi Darryl, I wondered if you didn't have plans for dinner can I shout your family some burgers at Dino's café up the road. It has a stunning view. Your family will enjoy it. To apologise for the lack of a barbecue.'

Our grandkids were excited by the idea, and our daughter had heard that Dino's was a great place for burgers. Before I'd had a chance to reply, there was another message from Sally: 'Absolute last thing we want is people being disappointed in their accommodation. We hope that people leave with happy memories not sad ones or disappointed ones.'

I texted back: 'Thank you Sally. We will take you up on that. We appreciate the gesture. 4 adults, 2 primary age children. Would 6pm suit?'

Peter Darmody

We'd expected Sally would be at Dino's when we arrived, but she'd simply booked a table in her name, and the staff knew she'd pick up the tab for the burgers. I realised then that she mightn't even live nearby.

We paid for our drinks and had an excellent meal. My Aussie Burger was so high the others were embarrassed to watch me eat it. Our grandkids stared at me in amazement over their burger n' chips and nachos.

Afterwards I texted Sally: *'Thank you very much Sally. Great burgers, great service, great view.'*

'Glad you enjoyed,' she replied. *'It's my fave spot. I've put on 7kg since I discovered it.'*

Having never set eyes on Sally, I could only speculate on what difference those seven kilos might have made.

On our last morning, I was thinking that although we'd all had a good time, particularly with the kayaks on the nearby lagoon, there were still some things they needed to fix, especially considering the fees they were charging. Some public comments on the booking site might push Sally and co. to do something.

Then a message arrived from Sally to all checking-out guests, ending with: *'If you have any ideas or suggestions that may have assisted making your stay more enjoyable, please will you let us know here rather than on a public platform that may affect our future guests' choices to stay here.'*

A dilemma, I thought, as I showed the message to the others. 'I'd come here again,' my daughter said. 'I don't think you should put anything critical on the booking site,' my wife added. Those two are always softer than me.

'OK,' I said, knowing I was beaten. And the truth was that we'd had a fun time over our four days, despite the house limitations. I sent my reply the next day, after we'd left:

'Hi Sally. We enjoyed our stay at beach house and would book it again. However, we'd like to suggest some small touches that would present the place better and make a stay even more enjoyable.'

I suggested a plug in the bathroom sink would be helpful, along with enough cereal/dessert bowls for the number of guests, and fixing the deep vehicle ruts at the entrance. *'Also,'* I said, *'the old shipping container and stack of weathered timber at the back of the house is probably not the best view for arriving guests. They make the place look a bit uncared for.'*

I didn't mention the BBQs, but thanked Sally once more for the burger gesture, and said we'd appreciated use of the kayaks.

There was a quick reply from Sally:

'Ha ha, you are totally right on all of this!! Thank you so much for your feedback. We appreciate every bit of it! I want to thank you for leaving the place so lovely for us. That poor house has worn so many storms, and needs bulldozing to be honest. Which is the plan after my property settlement with my ex.'

'TMI,' said my daughter. 'Too much information.'

But at least it explained why the place seemed a little run-down, and why Sally wasn't spending too much on 'peripherals'. But a plug for the bathroom sink and a few more cereal bowls didn't seem too much to ask.

'If she bulldozes it,' my daughter said with a laugh, 'she'll probably build a new place and charge even more for it.'

If we ever do book *Beach House* again, whether the old place or a new one, I'm going to hold Sally to her final promise. *'You will always be welcome back,'* she said, *'and another night at Dino's café will be on me.'*

I reckon we might go back. I wouldn't mind another one of those Aussie burgers.

---

*All names have been changed.

THEY DO NOT KNOW

(For my late mother, Peggy, who said that most people didn't know what it was like to live in wartime Brisbane. She was 17 when World War II began, 22 when the war in the Pacific ended.)

THEY DO NOT KNOW,
those who came after,
how the bugle call sounded
and the men went away;
when ration cards sold
in back streets of the city
and meat cost as much
as a single week's pay.

They do not know,
those with buds in their ears,
how we listened to rumours
of invasion to come;
how we lived with anxiety,
with gossip and blackouts,
and ran for the shelters
but refused to succumb.

They do not know,
those reaping high salaries,
how we once had sweet fun
on next-to-nought pay
in the arms of young soldiers
at dances and parties,
knowing the foe
was just islands away.

They do not know,
the punters and brokers,
how we bet on the future
with our wounded and dead;
not knowing if lovers
would ever come back to us,
not knowing if there were
more dark days ahead.

They do not know,
those planning their futures,
that there was a time
we had hopes and dreams too;
but our visions were clouded
by tears for the dying;
the best we could pray was
we'd all see it through.

They do not know,
those who came after,
of that unreal existence
when nothing was sure,
or why we still yearn
for missed fun and laughter
—those who grew up
when the world was at war.

Peter Darmody

OFFCUTS 3

WHAT DO YOU SAY TO A LIVING GODDESS?

'Come this way,' my Nepali colleague said. 'I want to show you something special.'

Prakash steered me towards a low open doorway in a white three-storeyed building with numerous black timber-framed windows. He spoke to a man at the door, then turned to me. 'We're in luck,' he said, taking my arm and urging me through the doorway. 'She should be here soon.'

We were in Hanuman Dhoka Durbar Square, in the centre of Kathmandu, capital city of Nepal. It was April 2024, and I was in the country for a month as a Visiting Scholar at Kathmandu University with Volunteers Australia. Prakash had just guided me around the ancient nine-storey royal palace, where kings had presided for generations. The 11th king of Nepal finally gave up power in 2006.

We emerged in a square courtyard onto a wide wooden verandah that ran around all four sides. The building reared above us, glazed red-brick walls with lots of the same sorts of dark timber-framed windows we'd seen on the outside, many of them with fine timber mesh hiding their interiors.

Other people filtered into the courtyard behind us, staring up at the windows. I looked inquiringly at Prakash.

He smiled. 'We're here to see Kumari, the living goddess.'

In the short time I'd been in Nepal, I'd seen lots of statues of Hindu and Buddhist gods and goddesses. Some were in small domestic and roadside shrines, some were large sculptures in prominent public places and temples. But I knew from my guides and reading that these gods and goddesses we're very much in the past. This was the first time I'd heard of a living goddess.

My mind reeled—what powers might a living goddess have? What place did she have in the lives of everyday Nepalese people? More importantly, what do you say when you meet a living goddess?

It seemed that Kumari was due to appear in the courtyard at 5:30 pm. Ten minutes to go. More people trickled in through the outside door. I had my camera at the ready, despite a prominent sign that said, *Taking photographs of Kumari is strictly prohibited.*

While we waited, Prakash told me the story of the living goddess. I'm relating it here to the best of my (outsider's) understanding.

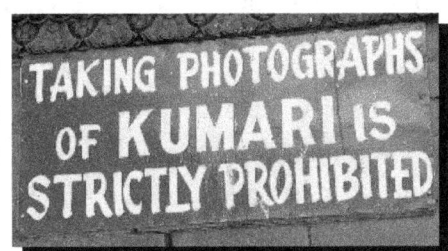

According to local beliefs, centuries ago a Buddhist goddess, Taleju, would often visit the ancient kings' palaces, where she played card games with them. One day, however, she had a dispute with one of the kings and disappeared. This king was very upset, and after many prayers begging her forgiveness, she appeared to him in a dream. Taleju told the king to choose a young Kumari (meaning *Princess*) whose body she would possess, and so live through that young woman as an ongoing living goddess.

Since that day, a young woman has been chosen from the high caste Shakya clan of the Nepalese community in Kathmandu to become the Kumari. Through a rigorous process, she is selected at about five or six years of age and remains a 'living goddess' until she attains puberty at around age 15. At that time the deity is said to vacate the young woman's body and she returns to normal life, to be replaced by a newly selected Kumari.

During the 10 or so years as a living goddess, Kumari does not leave her palace in the centre of the city except on a few ceremonial occasions during festivals. At these times she is transported around the city on a special golden palanquin, borne on strong men's shoulders. During her time in the palace, she apparently has family with her and private tutoring. It's said that once she enters the palace, Kumari's feet are not allowed to touch the floor because they are sacred. On one of her circuits of the city, to be able to touch her feet is supposed to bring good luck to any worshipper who gets close enough.

By now I was really intrigued to meet this living goddess. My hopes of a quick word and a selfie were dashed, however, when I learned that Kumari would not actually come into the courtyard, but would appear at one of the second-floor windows. A security guard pointed out the space to watch, a triple-arched window framed in the same dark timber.

There was a hush as 5:30 pm drew near. The light was good and the security men went around the small crowd making sure our cameras were put away. We all stared intently at the three windows above us, and I wondered what this carefully chosen young goddess would look like.

Next moment, a woman's face appeared at the window on the left of the set of three. I frowned. I thought Kumari was a young woman—this person looked to be about 60. She leaned forward, looking severe. 'No cameras,' she shouted.

Oh, this wasn't Kumari. This was her minder, making absolutely sure no one was taking photos. The security guards circled.

When they were positive there were no cameras in sight, a young woman appeared at the middle window. She was perhaps 12 or so, wearing a red top and a string of pearls around her neck. So, this was Kumari, the living goddess. She leaned on the window sill with folded arms and looked down at us. I think she was wearing red lipstick, but it was hard to take it all in. (Afterwards I learned from publicly available photos that when she's taken out on ceremonial occasions, her face and eyes are quite heavily made up.)

Peter Darmody

Offcuts 3

On this occasion, no one spoke. We stared at her and she stared at us. I was transfixed. Kumari didn't smile or wave. What did she make of this motley collection of tourists gathered in her courtyard where she was apparently obliged to appear daily on schedule? After a few minutes, the living goddess pulled back from the window and she and her minder disappeared. I wondered if her feet were touching the floor.

The security guards indicated it was time to leave, and I went back into the big square outside, trying to comprehend what I'd just seen. I turned to Prakash. 'When I came to Nepal a couple of weeks ago,' I said, my eyes wide open, 'I expected to experience a different culture to my own. But I had no idea I'd come face to face with a living goddess.'

Prakash smiled and nodded. He'd anticipated my reaction, and the occasion remains one of my strong memories from my short time in Nepal.

That evening I rang my wife back in Brisbane to tell her of my experience. She listened to me recount my story without comment.

'That's not the first living goddess you've met,' she said. 'Don't you realise you've been living with one for years?'

JEFF THORPE

HEADING WEST

On reflection, our west quest is many chaptered,
getting there has seen many travel modes adapted,
and quantifying 'west' means not only WA,
but Queensland, SA, Northern Territory on the way.
It began in '87 with Wimbledon winner Pat Cash
whose victory was broadcast in a news flash
while we viewed Uluru as backdrop for sunrise,
no colder morn have we felt, as I memorise.

Brian Goeldner

Offcuts 3

This was on a coach tour, tenting every night,
mum and dad and three kids on a trip to delight,
through western Qld, Territory and down to Port Augusta
an adventure which for city kids, an outback blockbuster.
We rode camels, climbed Uluru and slept underground
at Coober Pedy, camped at Devil's Marbles, vista to astound.
We flew over the Olgas and hiked all through Kings Canyon—
nothing more than striking scenery required for a companion.

By two thousand and five, the kids had left the nest,
'twas time to resume our interest in the west.
More up-market this visit to Perth and southern parts,
on to Margaret River famed for wine-making arts,
and a hike of a distance, not one seen as petty,
3.6 km return on historic Busselton Jetty.
Largest wooden pier in the southern Hemisphere,
with observatory and train, anything but austere.

Peter Darmody

July that year saw us captivated, touring the Kimberley,
sky and land and water merged in perfect synergy,
beehive domes of Purnululu, haunting Cathedral Cave
where a didgeridoo-player performer played in the nave.
Gorges, rock art, waterfalls, intense colours of Cape Leveque
from Kununurra to Broome, indeed nature's blank cheque.
The trip of a lifetime, one we never will forget,
such a little visited area, yet exceptional asset.

Brian Goeldner

Back west again in 06, to hail spouse's retirement.
life now saw more travel, almost a requirement,
with this trip extending to a leisurely four weeks
bush walks through wildflowers, scaling Porongurup peaks,
stays at Albany and Esperance amidst their glorious beaches,
gleaming sand and turquoise water their top features.
Then back to Perth for Red Bull Air Race, downright electrifying,
death-defiant stunts by pilots needing certifying.

Offcuts 3

Come twenty-o-eight on the move, the west won out again,
two excursions realised, neither one mundane
launching in South Australia early in the year,
a month or so's visit on days scorching and clear,
riding bikes on Clare rail trail, tasting wine along the way,
the commanding Flinders Ranges, nirvana on display,
Makybe Diva's statue, tall on Port Lincoln's shore,
Eyre and Yorke Peninsulas, treasure troves and more.

May back in Queensland on a Happy Wanderer's tour,
three weeks camping to places well-known and obscure,
Longreach and Winton, to home of Crocodile Dundee,
Cloncurry, Gulflander train and Karumba by the sea.
Explored Undara lava tubes and Chillagoe limestone caves,
where sundry stalactites performed the role of architraves.
Skilled in tent logistics by end of this trip,
well-versed on when and what to zip or unzip.

Twenty-fifteen heading west once more, unable to abstain
this time on the lavish Indian Pacific train,
haute cuisine on rails, a bed on which to sleep at night.
We embarked at Sydney, Broken Hill stop at first light
Adelaide next halt after sampling Barossa Valley.
two days before Perth for further tasting from the galley.
However, all came to an end while on the Nullabor,
derailment on the line ahead, we could proceed no more.

But the appetite was whetted for travel on the rails.
Next year we tried the Westlander at the speed of snails:
Charleville the destination, where we'd never been before
and truly, what a surprise that town had in store.
Superb Cosmos night sky show, bilby presentation
plus, fascinating tales of US war participation,
coupled with comical history of Corones hotel
made the trip to Charleville go down very well.

Westlander: www.outbackqueensland.com.au/rail-experiences

On to twenty-seventeen and another journey west
by Spirit of the Outback, no need for Sunday best.
Summer fares of 'two for one' made the trip appealing,
no helter-skelter on this train, just peaceful calm
    freewheeling.
And this, I guess, reflects a change of attitude to travel,
where what was relished years ago would today unravel.
Twenty-one days tenting now, I think would cause divorce,
but add up the memories and there's no trace of remorse.

John Brown

JOHN AND THE RAINBOW PRINCESS

IN THE 1840S MY ANCESTORS were pioneers in Coleraine, Victoria, where they set up their own settlement and called it Brown Town. They had 16 children who also had big families. I was a third-generation descendant and, at the age of nineteen, I believed that there was more in life than hard work.

I was seeking a soulmate to share my earthly journey, and every time I told Mum she would say, 'Don't go near her, she's your cousin.' So this is what sent me to Queensland to find true love. I found work share-farming on the Darling Downs.

Satisfied that I had played my part in the win, I left my team mates celebrating the Rugby League victory that gave us the premiership. I jumped on my trusted motor bike and navigated my way along the potholed gravel road on the way back to my share dairy farm to milk the cows before going to the Saturday night dance at the Felton Hall.

As I reached the crest of the hill on the tree-lined Pittsworth-Felton road, I saw a brilliant rainbow stretched across the Felton valley, its background of black cloud capped with a white veil shawl on its shoulders. A panoramic view of the beautiful valley, with its scattered farm houses, green pastures and fallowed wheat fields ready for planting, caught my attention, as did the little village with a dance hall, church, cheese factory and small grocery store. A wide-winged eagle hovered overhead, as frolicking birds in their thousands partied in the after-the-rain clear blue sky, adding to my lasting memory of the ambience of this special close-family-living community.

I stopped and stood by the bike for a while in awe and contemplation and took in the beautiful moments as the rainbow ends passed over Mt Rubieslaw and the gap between the adjacent hills. It painted a magnificent picture when the ends passed over my farm as a beautiful rainbow half-moon arch.

Football was no longer on my mind, but rather a thought that there was a beautiful young debutante sitting on the verandah with a vision that a handsome prince was about to sweep her away over the rainbow and give her a life of love and adventure.

I had changed my milk factory sales to the local cheese factory at Felton, the little settlement about five miles down the road. Whereas before I would have to take my milk out to the road, the carrier now came to the farm to collect it. The milk truck driver, a married man with six children and five more to come, was responsible for my attendance at the Felton Hall dance. Ken whet my already established desire for romance, telling me about all the beautiful girls who would be there and, in particular, a stunning blonde.

I had previously gone to Cambooya and Drayton for my dances and, when introduced to the Felton girls by our cupid-like truck driver, I was more than impressed. My cupid had done his homework and primed the girls on his milk pickup rounds, telling them that a new Casanova would be at the dance.

On the right there was a striking blonde, in the middle a pretty young brunette teenage girl with hair down to her shoulders, and on the left five teenage beauties that would catch the eye of any hot-blooded man. Who would I choose to ask for the first dance?

I had set my sights on the brunette, but was beaten to the post by a red-headed bloke, so I quickly headed for the blonde, cutting ahead of one of the other lads. We chatted and flirted a bit and, when the dance was over, I escorted her back to her seat and took up a position that gave me an advantage over the redhead.

The Pride of Erin announcement saw me first this time and, as I asked the brunette to dance, I saw a beautiful smile, not knowing that I would treasure many more over the next sixty-five years. We didn't get another dance that night as I felt I should give them all a chance to know the new boy in the mix. However I did have a second dance with the blonde when the MC announced the ladies' choice and she chose me.

I was sometimes reminded in later banter that I had eyes only for the blonde and danced mostly with her. In return, I reminded Ailsa that, when her friend Esme asked her what she thought of 'that fellow Brown' she said, 'Not much.' I also teased her that a red-headed chap often had her up dancing when I was late coming back into the hall, after being held up while swapping yarns with the boys as we waited for the next dance.

A decision to cease milk pick-up by the factory made it necessary for me to look for a suitable vehicle to cart my milk. So I purchased my first four-wheel motor vehicle, a rag hood Whippet utility that had been cut down from a sedan.

One cold winter night I intended to go to the dance at Cambooya until I reached the farm gate and had a change of mind that took me to the dance at Leyburn. It was a case of serendipity triggering off a beautiful soulmate relationship destined to last a lifetime and a partnership that gave us three beautiful children and seven grandchildren and ten great grandchildren. It led Ailsa and me from humble beginnings to a life of fulfillment that allowed us to see Australia and a fair bit of the world.

I had chosen to ride my motor bike and entered the dance hall nearly frozen to the bone. I warmed up at the unexpected sight of the stunning brunette from Felton on whom I had set my sights. Ailsa was sitting with her cousin Bob and his girlfriend Esme, and greeted me with a beautiful smile and an invitation to sit with them. We danced the night away, me in a state of euphoria. The night was over when I escorted her to Bob's car where, after accepting my request to save the first dance for me at the next Felton dance, Ailsa quickly jumped in and gave me a goodnight wave—the first kiss would have to wait.

However, at the next dance there was no sign of Ailsa, and at the end of the first two segments I chose the blonde. Half-way through, in walked Ailsa with her cousin Bob and his girlfriend Esme. She blamed Esme for holding them up.

By the end of the night we were friends again. Although I was a bit subdued early, I issued an invitation to take her home and was more than pleased when my invitation was accepted. My Whippet had a rag hood and no side curtains, and was no carriage for a lovely young lady. I think it was Esme who named it the *Windy Whippet*. I had a big leather coat that I gave to my passenger, and I wore an air force wrap-around coat, so apart from the ears and face, cold wasn't a problem. (If you haven't lived on the Darling Downs, it's hard to understand just how cold a frosty night can get.)

As we arrived at the residence, *Ailron*, Ailsa was out of the car in a flash and inside the gate before I could do the gentleman act and open the door for her. Once inside the gate she kept me talking in the cold for quite a while.

I was having problems with the green-eyed monster, the red-haired rival, and other blokes like the budding farmers awaiting their inheritance and offering a better life.

One of the ladies who had been so good to Ailsa after her mother died had her heart set on one of her two boys being the prize-winner and, when the handsome Rodney turned up with a homemade picnic case for her, I knew I'd better lift my game. I have a few trophies and a couple of premierships at football and cricket and worked hard for them, but to have Ailsa as my wife was the biggest trophy I would ever have and I was focused on achieving just that.

I thought a way to impress her was to give her a few eggs from my recently purchased pullets that had just started laying. After milking on a cold night after a rainy couple of days, I wasn't able to drive the Whippet to the road because it would bog on the mud track. But I had no intention of missing out on an invite to dinner.

I chose to try the motor bike as it had better traction on the wet tracks. With half a dozen pullet eggs in my sports jacket, I hit a puddle on the mud track on the way out to the gate. In saving myself from a buster, some of the eggs broke, and I arrived a bit embarrassed. Some of the eggs were only shell-cracked and would be used for scrambled eggs on toast for a GC (her father) breakfast next morning.

From then on it was regular dates for the dances and a night at the pictures under the chaperoning eyes of Bob and Esme, prompting a warning from my future father-in-law to be careful of someone coming from interstate calling himself John Brown.

Not long afterwards I changed to a 1934 Ford Sedan. This was a more comfortable way of taking Ailsa to dances, but we still held fond memories of what Ess had named the *Windy Whippet*. With the Felton boys there was an arrangement that we took it in turns with our cars to pick up the girls and drive to the district dances— me with the Ford and the others borrowing their parents' car. Sometimes we had up to eight people squeezed into the bench seats; no seatbelt in the cars back then.

In the earlier stages of getting to know each other I asked Ailsa to a dance at Pittsworth. She was always one to put others first, so she went to get in the back, which would have left the front seat vacant for the blonde with whom (as with the other girls) I had enjoyed a dance or two. Encouraged by Ess and me, Ailsa took her rightful place and kept the dreaded flighty blonde at bay.

One day Bob, Ess and Ailsa had gone early to the night session of the Carnival of Flowers in Toowoomba, and I had arranged to meet them at the Town Hall. This was another highlight of our romance—choosing to see a movie at the Empire Theatre in Margaret Street. It was the night of our first kiss.

We later sometimes went there with our children before we left Toowoomba. However I hadn't been back for over forty years until, through my Men's Shed, I received two complimentary tickets to a live Paul Hogan Show. The memories we shared on that night bring tears to my eyes.

The rest of 1951 saw us at weekly dances, card parties and celebration occasions, most of which I was invited to by Ailsa and my new Felton friends. Felton folk were a friendly lot, accepting me, a stranger, into their fold. Rodney and the red-headed rival had seen the writing on the wall and were no longer a threat.

It was nearing Christmas and we had been in severe drought. Most of my cows had dried up, so I decided that I would need to leave my few milk cows to my neighbour to enable him to supplement his supply to the factory while I sought other income.

As my cows were not due to start calving until March I dried them off and took a six-week break at Coleraine, working with my brothers in their truck transport enterprise. It was a hard decision for Ailsa and me, but we were confident that we would resume our romance on my return. I flew to Coleraine, working hard with my brothers, and every night reading and writing a few very special letters.

At last the six weeks were up, and having worked hard I had a bit more money than when I left. I enjoyed my stay at Coleraine, but my heart was now firmly in Queensland. I returned to a warm welcome. When I arrived back I headed for that little place with its beautiful girl. She was there to greet me at the gate and invite me in, her father now convinced that the Victorian calling himself John Brown was there for the long haul. The cows began to calve and the drought broke about the same time, so 1952 was a good year for me, allowing me to pay off my debts and buy some good clothes.

We announced our engagement on 11 July that year and just after this I went down with what I thought at the time was a bad flu, but now believe was a dose of Q Fever as no one else, including Ailsa, who nursed me, contracted the malady.

I would crawl out of bed and struggle through the milking, clean up the dairy then take the milk to the factory and on the way home call at Ailsa's place and sleep until time to do the evening milking. Then to bed and fitfully sleep all night. It was a dreadful week or ten days for me and it took a while for me to recover.

Felton and my cows and a good season with regular rain saw me in a better place to offer Ailsa a future, but only through love and faith could we make our marriage work. When I proposed, I said something like, 'All I have to offer you is me and the love I have for you.'

We both knew it was coming, but even with our excitement, fronting her father GC was not easy. As a widower, what would he do without his daughter's help in coming years?

The problem was solved when, seeing the writing on the wall, he decided to retire from share-farming and buy a beautiful old Queenslander on top of a ridge overlooking the town of Pittsworth. The house was next to his son Ron, and ideal for Ron to keep an eye out for their welfare. They moved in just before Christmas, and Ailsa lived in it with her brother Frank and Pa, until a week before our wedding.

We cemented our commitment to each other at Picnic Point, Toowoomba, with a ring I gave her on 10 July 1952, and announced our engagement next day, with Aunty May throwing a party.

We put the wedding forward from the planned Easter week-end to the earlier date of 31 January because my cows were due for calving early March, and financially we needed to be back from our honeymoon for the full production. Neighbour Bob would milk my cows and keep the money for the milk while we were away.

It was a special time for Ailsa, making the plans for the wedding and enjoying the parties thrown for her by her Aunty May and friends. It was also a busy time for me, having replaced the 1934 Ford sedan with a Prefect utility, only to find that I needed to replace the crankshaft big-end bearings a fortnight before the wedding. This was achieved only two days prior, thanks to the help of Bob Hanlon, a dear friend who was keen to help after my previous assistance in getting his house ready for his bride several months earlier.

I had arranged to pick Ailsa up at Pittsworth and take her to her Aunty May for the week before the wedding. I had been busy working on the Prefect and when I turned up in clothes covered in grease at nine o'clock, I imagined I saw doubt in her mind: *What am I getting myself into?* But the tasty meal she served me cleared any doubts.

On the first day of our honeymoon, after breakfast at the hotel in Warwick we headed south. For the first time in her life Ailsa had her taste of another State, this being the first but certainly not the last of her travels to all states and territories in Australia.

The little Prefect was running well, and we made Glen Innes for a morning tea break. I was finished filling up with petrol and, looking up when Ailsa came towards me, my heart leapt as I realised that this was my beautiful wife, and with a hug I told her so.

We camped by the roadside in the back of the utility under our crude canopy for the rest of our wonderful honeymoon, travelling through four states. Everything was fine until we broke a crown and pinion, and that replacement cost us a third of our honeymoon money. Fortunately, the rest of the way was free of mechanical mishap. However, our progress was slow because our Prefect was not able to pass the slow-moving trucks uphill.

Any time we managed to get past they overtook us on the flats, leaving us with the passing problem on the next rise.

Ailsa had always wanted to swim at Bondi Beach, and we had a few precious hours there before an overnight stay camped on the banks of the Murrumbidgee River at Gundagai. An off-course diversion to the Hume Weir was a highlight on our way over the border into Victoria, then on to Violet Town for our overnight camp before proceeding, accompanied by Ailsa's uncertainty about meeting my parents.

A stop for a freshen-up at the Wannon River Falls had her in a less nervous state, and that nervousness soon went when we were met with a shower of confetti on our arrival. I had a precious moment with Mum when in a hug I managed to whisper, 'And she's not my cousin.'

The week of reunion for me while Ailsa got to know her new family and friends was over all too soon, and we left for a visit to Mt Gambier to see its beautiful lakes and caves. In the late afternoon we stopped for another bush camp, this time at Port Fairy. The next day we travelled along the Great Ocean Road and on through Melbourne to Hastings and my sister Isa and her five children. We stayed there for a couple of days, on one of which we caught a steam train to Flinders Station.

Ailsa had often spoken of her wish to travel on an electric train, so after a look around the city we caught the only one in Melbourne at that time. Another dream come true and another promise kept. We enjoyed our day out, and travelled to the northern suburbs and back before getting the normal train back to Isa's place.

Time was beginning to run out and we would need to be getting back to the cows and crops, so we bid our farewell and travelled through Gippsland to a camp on the Cooma River, with only a few stops along the way, including a swim at Lakes Entrance.

Anyone who has had the dubious pleasure of driving along the Bonang-Bonang Highway when it was gravel and before some of the bends were taken out would know why we spent some of our dwindling money on a penny ice-cream at Delegate.

We arrived at the Cooma River in the twilight and chose a secluded spot, though it was unlikely anyone would be on that road at that time of day. It had been a hot day and we were covered in dust and ready for a nuddy swim in the clear flowing stream before our meal. My memory lets me down regarding our meals on the way, but in our sixty-three years of married life she never gave me one I didn't enjoy, so I'm sure they were great.

We spent some time in Canberra and then set our sails for home again, camping along the way, and arriving home to begin the rest of a journey of love and adventure. Ahead for us there was a life of commitment, children and world travel beyond our dreams. Two people from humble backgrounds and a faith ready to broaden their horizons and have a God-blessed purposeful life.

The eagle prince from Brown Town had swooped into the sleepy Felton valley and plucked his princess, ready to take her to a life she had dreamed of—on the night of the beautiful Rainbow.

Dave Shearer

HOLIDAY ADVENTURES ON THE COORONG, SOUTH AUSTRALIA

THE COORONG AREA in South Australia is a long shallow lagoon, approximately 1.2 metres deep, some 100 kilometres long, separated from the Southern Ocean by the dunes of the Younghusband Peninsula. They brag about the natural beauty, abundant wildlife, unspoilt coastline and the variety of pelicans along the coast, which rule the roost.

My connection with the Coorong started in the late 1950s. My family travelled down from Adelaide southeast to a camping area at Policeman's Point, situated halfway down the Coorong, for our annual holidays. Policeman's Point is a historic site—in the early days the mounted police used it as an overnight camping area, hence the name. The accommodation was simple wooden cabins with bunk beds, kitchen table and chairs, cold showers and long-drop toilets.

So, we settled into a relaxing holiday, swimming in the Coorong and lots of walks. During our stay my parents made friends with the owners of the park, the Deed family, plus I made a friendship with their son John, who was a couple of years older than me. So this led to future trips back down there in later years.

I ended up going out with John rabbiting, as he earned money trapping rabbits and selling them on to butcher shops. He set up 40–50 traps per night, then ran them in the morning, cleaned the bunnies' stomachs out and took them down to the mobile refrigeration truck. They were then transported to bigger towns to be processed. The meat ended up in butchers' shops and the skins or fur was used to make hats. Back then it was common to serve up roasted rabbit for meals.

The Deeds also worked the Coorong for fish. They ran two flat-bottom boats, complete with extended long-shafted outboard motors to move in shallow waters. The family used fishing nets for their catch, and the fish too were transported to town for sale.

In the years that followed I returned on my own during school holidays via the bus that travelled from Adelaide to Mount Gambier, and stayed with the Deed family. John took me out kangaroo shooting, which was very exciting for a city lad. We always brought the meat home to cook up for meals and food for the dogs. Dawn Deed, John's mother, always cooked up tasty kangaroo roast with vegetables.

My father bought me a small .22 rifle, so I joined in with John on our shooting trips in later years. We ventured across the Coorong in John's fishing boat and climbed the large sandhills on

Younghusband Peninsula, then down to the Southern Ocean front. I remember the beach was so long it disappeared into the horizon.

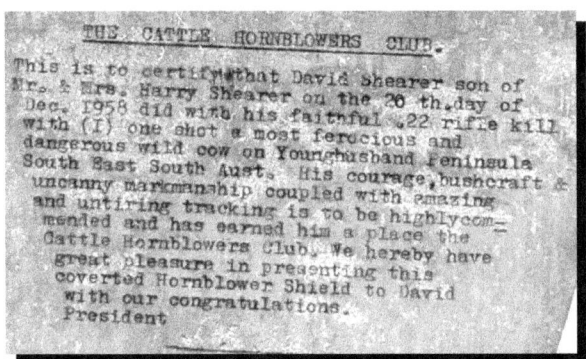

On one of our trips across the peninsula we came across a wild cow. Since we were carrying our rifles, we both took aim. I won the trophy for the day, as I downed the cow in one shot. John was very impressed! We cut the rear legs off and brought them back for a cook-up later. We also cut off one of the horns and brought that back too, which John's father used to make me a special trophy to take home.

The full length of the Coorong is now a national park. My memories of these holidays in that part of South Australia have stayed with me over the years and our friendship has also remained.

ROCK AND ROLL

It's not every day one gets to ride a navigational buoy, especially while floating amongst the waves. The hardest part is to get aboard, and the weather conditions always dictate this. As a lighthouse mechanic this was one of your maintenance duties. When you found out it was on the jobs list for the day, you immediately rolled your eyes and thought, *Here we go again, hang on!*

The lighthouse department operated its own boat or had a local boat on contract to transport us out to the buoys. As usual, it was the weather conditions on the particular day of inspection that said yes or no. Also, it was the boat captain's responsibility not only to safeguard the lighthouse mechanic, but also not to damage the boat or the buoy. I can remember attempting the task three days in a row before finally getting on to the buoy!

On arrival, the challenge was to assess if it was calm enough to step off the boat directly on to the buoy or instead tie a car tyre over the bow, hanging from the handrail, just above the water. The more exciting experience was via the car tyre.

One would carefully climb over the side using the handrail and then attempt to place one foot onto the tyre. When this was accomplished, the boat would be carefully manoeuvred towards the buoy and spare the thought they would ever touch together. When the gap was right, you stretched one leg out ready to land on the buoy, plus one arm to grab the buoy superstructure. As the buoy swung over towards the boat, you quickly made a grab and then held on for your life! Then as the buoy swung back the other way, it sucked you off the boat and you hung on tight to prepare for a heavy landing. You also carried a leather bag of tools on your back to do the maintenance check.

Landing on the buoy, you scrambled up the steel ladder to the top where the gas lantern was mounted. You then carefully positioned yourself, feet on the ladder rung and your back against a tubular handrail with the lantern in front of you. The top section of the lantern was then opened up on a hinge to give access to the flasher unit inside. An inspection was then carried out. Also, a gas pressure gauge was fitted to the acetylene gas pipe which came up from the two gas cylinders mounted in the body of the buoy.

Offcuts 3

While all this work was being carried out, the buoy swayed from side to side with the wave action of that day. If you suffered from seasickness, the job was not for you. With the inspection completed, the lantern was locked up and then it was back down the ladder. The boat then came back in, your leg was out again, arm stretched out in readiness to leave the buoy.

So, another buoy inspection was carried out by the lighthouse service to assist the master mariners from across the world to a safe trip around our Australian coastline.

JEFF THORPE

THE KOOLAMA AFFAIR

MANY KIMBERLEY CRUISES visit Koolama Bay
to admire the twin waterfalls of King George River,
no doubt cruise passengers are informed of the affray
of M V Koolama and the bombs Japs did deliver.

A 4,000 tonne vessel carrying passengers and freight
Koolama was owned by W A State Shipping Service;
launched in 1938, it did not deserve the fate
to become four years later a war casualty on purpose.

10 February 1942 Koolama sailed from Fremantle, Darwin
    bound,
One-eighty on board including 14 soldiers and 90 crew,
ten days later, in a manner profound
war reached Koolama in a terrifying coup.

MV Koolama: https://navyhistory.au/the-koolama-incident

Eighteen bombs were dropped by three Japanese aircraft,
four struck *Koolama* causing grim damage to her stern,
knocking out her steering, severely affecting her draft,
leaving her unseaworthy as crew were soon to learn.

No fatalities and injuries sparse but, their position dire,
35k from land, three hundred from Wyndham, nearest port,
luckily sea was calm and although piloting gone haywire,
Koolama limped to Cape Rulhieres, beaching as last resort.

Lifeboats transferred most from ship to nearby Calamity Bay
later renamed 'Koolama' after the boat,
Captain Egglestone with skeleton crew worked to find a way
to undertake repair enough to keep the ship afloat.

Koolama Bay, WA (Photo: Peter Darmody)

Chief Officer Reynolds oversaw those on shore,
fresh water available from waterfall and stores on board,
need for food and drink thus, in short-term catered for
yet, rescue seemed unlikely, Broome and Darwin floored.

Contact was made with Benedictine Monks, Drysdale River
    Mission
100k from Koolama Bay through rough, rugged terrain;
a lugger was dispatched, aboriginal runners in addition
to chiefly collect those injured and most in pain.

Egglestone and Reynolds argued how to solve their plight,
near mutiny ensued from reports of those around;
the Captain chose re-floating and sail to Wyndham despite
anger from many, afraid attack would see people drowned.

Ultimate outcome saw survival by a variety of means,
on February 25 the lugger transported sick and injured to
    the Mission,
next day ninety-three set out overland, aborigines as screens,
those deemed fit enough to undertake transition.

01 March saw patched up *Koolama* sail for Wyndham on
    high tide,
twenty-eight crew arriving there next day,
a haphazard voyage before ship to wharf was tied
though pumps still required to float her where she lay.

On 03 March Wyndham suffered a Japanese air raid,
Koolama left unattended while the crew ran for cover,
mud clogging pumps saw crude repairs come unmade,
the ship rolled, capsized and sank, never to recover.

Offcuts 3

By March 06 those still at Koolama Bay were evacuated by
    seaplane
flying from Broome and landing on the bay,
doubtless pleased to depart the wilderness domain
which, from all accounts, remains untouched to this day.

In 1946 salvage was attempted to shift *Koolama* from the pier
to present no danger to other shipping,
moving the wreck 100 metres, keeping the channel clear,
she settled in deep water with mud bottom gripping.

A little-known war episode in remote part of the continent
remarkably, lives lost numbered merely one,
three plaques cemented on to rocks the only monument,
Australia put on notice close combat had begun.

Graham Trimble

GROWING UP – REAL FAST

THERE HAVE BEEN A NUMBER of events in my life that have meant I've had to grow up quickly.

The first of these was in 1955, when my father died. I was ten years old. We were living at Ouyen in dry and sandy north-western Victoria, and I remember going along to the cremation, not knowing exactly what it was. But I guess I did know it wasn't going to be in a coffin. And then realising, as the coffin quietly began to sink down, that this was about to come to an end, that for my father in the coffin it would only be ashes after that.

Another growing-up experience was with my seven siblings, four brothers and three sisters. The two older brothers slept in a sleepout, a room beside the bedroom that I and my two younger brothers slept in. The three sisters, all younger than the five boys, slept in the house. And it must have been that John, who's the second eldest in the family, had bullied us enough times that we decided—I and my two younger brothers, so it was probably instigated by me being the eldest of the three—'We'll get back at John, we'll call him "Johnny Appleseed".'

We used to call him that early on Sunday morning, when we knew he'd still be in his pyjamas. And we used to call him that until he really just went quite mental and he'd start chasing us, and we'd run off down the street in this little farming town, knowing that he wasn't going to run all the way after us because of his pyjamas.

We kind of got back at him, and I suppose in terms of growing up I began to learn you can defend yourself sometimes just with words—you don't have to go hitting anybody.

However, two young boys who used to kick us when we all turned up for Sunday School, we gave them a hiding. We chased them over a hill, and onto a reservoir. We caught them down in an irrigation channel. Then, I remember that Sunday afternoon after lunch their father coming up to our father, and having a 'chat'; we were looking around from behind the hedge. I don't remember how that finished up, but I do remember learning you can defend yourself if you work as a little group, and you can do it physically if you have to. Again it was just a part of growing up as a kid, having siblings that could help defend you against stuff, either verbal or physical.

Trimble family

After our father died, our mother decided in 1955 she'd buy a house in Huntly, near Bendigo, in central Victoria, which is 316 kilometres from Ouyen. Her mother, our grandmother, had a shop in Ouyen and, even though my mother inherited the farm from our father, together with its mortgage, she decided to move closer to our four uncles and three aunties on Dad's side of the family—Mum being a single child.

We used to drive down to Huntly and back from Ouyen while she was getting the purchased house ready; builders adding a sleepout on the back for her eight fatherless children. We'd be going back to Ouyen at night, and because my mother was an epileptic on 'heavy' medications, she'd sometimes go to sleep or doze off whilst driving. So as a kid, in this 1947 Chevrolet with my seven siblings, as I held on to the rail on the back of the front bench seat, driver's side, it was my task to talk to mum in her left or right ear: 'The road turns right here, Mum, turns left here, Mum.' I'd try to wake her up if I felt she was wobbling on the road a bit. So that was a growing-up experience too.

It's not an exaggeration to say that on those country roads, unlike today's highways, the gravel on the sides of the road often contained old nails and bits of wire in amongst the stones. We would have at least one puncture on every trip down to Bendigo and one on the way back.

When my grandmother died in 1960, my mother returned to Ouyen to run the shop. It was a haberdashery shop: men's wear, women's wear, underwear, and travel goods. She left me at Huntly in charge of my five younger siblings. The two older boys, Roy and John, stayed on at Ouyen to do their secondary schooling there. Because mum didn't know what her timetable would be when she took over my grandmother's shop and its staff, she had Roy and John boarded out in a house not far from the high school. She stayed in our grandmother's house, where she could come and go at will, and could come back down to Huntly to check on us.

1960.
5 SIBLINGS
GRAHAM TRIMBLE.

So that was a growing experience, that we were batching. Sometimes we'd run out of briquettes or wood, so I started working at weekends as a 13 year-old farm labourer to pay the power bills, and to get money for briquettes. I didn't have enough money sometimes. We did not know how long our mother would be away. I'd cut 24 rounds of sandwiches each day for my brothers' and sisters' lunches—vegemite and cheese, vegemite and bananas, honey and peanut butter, or sultanas and peanut butter. Great ingredients.

At high school I used to envy the kids who had money and could go down the street and buy baked beans on toast. I eventually found out that some of them would have loved to have had some of the sandwiches I was making. So they swapped their money for sandwiches, and I'd go down the street and buy baked beans on bloody toast! Gee, I loved it.

I mucked around at school and failed Year 10 (Intermediate). *Whew!* That caught me unprepared, because it meant I was going to be in a class, in Year 10 again, with one of my brothers. And that put a dent in my pride. On the second attempt I passed 12 subjects at Intermediate level, as opposed to a normal student passing with eight or nine.

The learning experience in all that was mathematics. I was doing maths again, and it had always been a big struggle for me. I'm not exaggerating—all of a sudden it was the 'aha' stage. It actually clicked in April of that second year at Year 10 (Form 4: Intermediate Level)—algebra, geometry, trigonometry. It kind of married itself together. I could see it was another language—as most adults come to understand, maths is a digital language-in-itself. That was a fantastic learning experience, and I have used it in my teaching career to inspire—'There's hope for you,' I'd say to struggling students.

In this decade (the 2010s) and during all the previous ones while I was teaching, I tried to inspire students by telling them that I failed Year 10. But I pulled my horns in, knuckled down, and went off to Dookie Agricultural College. This was just the most influential and memorable experience of all, and it was in agriculture. Dookie was a bit over 6000 acres (2,432 hectares) in size, comprising large sheep and beef cattle numbers, together with Cereal Cropping, Poultry Branch, Piggery Branch, Dairy and Milking Branch, Horticulture Branch, and Stock Branch. It was a monstrous learning experience after growing up with parents who farmed 1,500 acres (607 hectares). At age fifteen I applied and sat an exam to join the Navy and the Commonwealth Bank. I failed in maths for the Navy and chose not to become a Cadet in the Bank, to work in Melbourne.

Offcuts 3

I had started Year 11 at Bendigo High School. The father of one of the students I'd been in Year 10 with had a plumbing contract for the new buildings being built at Dookie Agricultural College. My mate said, 'Come for a drive up with my dad,' and we went up for a trip with him. Later at school one day in February of the next year, this friend said to me, 'I'm not going to go to Dookie. There's a spot because my dad booked me in. If you're interested, go and ring them up.'

I went down to the principal's office, and I asked him to ring the college to see if they would admit me. And then to ring my mother, who was back in Ouyen, 300 kms away, to obtain her authority. It was okay. Off I went to Dookie. It was a three-year diploma, which is equivalent to the second year if you do a degree in agriculture at a university.

SPORTS UNION COMMITTEE 1964
Left to Right: P. Martin, N. Duckworth, R. Helliwell, B. Mar, I. Speedie, L. Brooks, E. Denovan, G. Trimble, A. Botsman, C. Burbury.

At Dookie, we had a room of our own, our own heater, group shower facilities with unlimited hot water, our own bed, our own desk, bookshelves, cupboard, bookshelves and rubbish bin. At 7:30 am it was down for breakfast—you could eat as much as you like, you even got second servings. Each fortnight across those three years was divided into practical farm work, plus lectures, on alternate days. If the prac work you were assigned (one of seven branches: dairy, poultry, piggery, stock branch, horticulture, etc.) was a wet branch, meaning if you'd got to milk cows, assigned to feed pigs, or work in the poultry section, you had breakfast at a different time. Two hours later than normal, you'd have three or four eggs on your plate, rashes of bacon, tomatoes—you could go and get seconds if needed. It was amazing.

Fifty years later one of my teaching colleagues who came into my second year at Dookie Agricultural College—he was out of a teachers' college where there was always a bursary or studentship for primary school teachers wanting to teach in P-12 schools—wrote a letter to my eldest daughter. He said, 'I never realised it about your father that Dookie provided him with unlimited food.' To supplement our food we would go down in the night—and raid the almonds, or other seasonal fruits out of the horticulture orchard, or we'd break into the sweet corn, or we'd go into the poultry sheds and knock off eggs. It could almost bring tears to my eyes as I think about the enjoyment those three years Dookie College gave me.

All this well-supplied good food meant, in comparison to my family life, I developed from a skinny runt—to use an agriculture term—into a body capable of shearing sheep, using a crow-bar, working long hours at hard practical farm work and sports, like swimming, cross-country running, cycling and gymnastics.

I involved myself daily in gymnastics training. I noticed I was not good enough at AFL football or sprinting, but in bike-riding and gymnastics I trained hard and often. I became the College Gymnastics Champion two years in a row. I just loved that sport, eventually competing in the King of Mount Wycheproof, carrying a 64 kg bag of wheat, aged 35+. What a learning experience that was.

There were four terms at Dookie College, and exams at the end of each term. Of the 14 subjects I had to pass to get into second year, I failed eight of them at the Midyear Exams. That was a bit like a slap on the face. 'You better wake up, Graham, you can't go mucking around and still get a pass here,' I said to myself. 'Choose one or the other—muck around or study and work.'

I changed and excelled, making sure I shone at practical work, gymnastics, and throwing the javelin. But I wanted to make sure I passed other subjects as well, and I did. I was always maybe one-third up from the bottom, but at the end of the third year I got a special prize for my practical work with the HYPAR pigs (Hysterectomy Produced Artificially Reared).

At the end of three years at Ag College I graduated and went straight into teaching. I was teaching physics, maths, science and woodwork at Warragul Technical Secondary School, 106 km south-east of Melbourne, Victoria. The agricultural qualification was sufficient to get me into teaching, with a proviso, as the principal reminded me: 'If you want to become a permanent teacher, Graham, you're going to have to go out into industry.' It wouldn't matter if you came off a farm or went to an ag college—if you were trained in agriculture, you had to go out and work in the industry post your qualification, and then you could apply to go to teachers' college, which is what I did.

When I was teaching at Warragul in that first year out of Dookie, nearly every weekend I would hitchhike up to Bendigo (260 kilometres) every Friday straight after school. (I hitchhiked for about four or five years—I had my licence, but I didn't have enough money and I couldn't justify borrowing money to get a vehicle.) Sunday afternoon I'd hitchhike back to Warragul. On Tuesday nights, straight after school I'd hitchhike into Melbourne, 100 kilometres away. I'd go to the YMCA gymnastics club. I competed for them in the state competition.

At the end of that session (maybe 8 o'clock), I'd go for a swim, have a meal with one of my brothers in Melbourne, then hitchhike back to Warragul in the middle of the night, sometimes relying on the 2 am or 4 am milk truck. Back to school teaching by 8 am on the Wednesday. Then, on Thursday evening and night I did the same thing again, ready for teaching on Friday. I trained two nights a week at the YMCA in Melbourne for 10 or 11 months of the year, except during school holidays when I worked on farms in Victoria's Mallee Region.

I got into track cycling. Oh, that was another big learning phase. I learned to love match riding on the track, matching against another guy. Where you could feign behaviour, touch them—not allowed to elbow them or knee them, even though your legs are going up and down like pistons. But the speed of it and balancing up on the slope. That was almost as good as gymnastics—but not quite. I did that in Warragul—got a special gift from the Warragul

Cycling Club for encouraging cycling in the school. I've also raced at Bendigo, Echuca, Maryborough, Morwell, Bairnsdale and Brunswick in Melbourne.

I did 12 months teaching at Warragul, then one year with the Department of Agriculture as a Technical Officer and research guy up at the Mallee Research Station (Walpeup). Then I went shearing in New South Wales and, if it was wet, driving a tractor for a farmer and his son. I did a bit of fencing. That was full time, all-up for those two years, and then I went down to Melbourne to Toorak Technical Teachers' College for one-year's teacher training. That was two-and-a-half days in the week doing lectures, and two-and-a-half days teaching at Box Hill Technical Secondary School.

After I graduated and before I took up my first teacher posting, I got married. Meeting Jan and getting married was brilliant—a bit like the Dookie experience, beautiful and rewarding. We courted for four years, didn't go out with anyone else, then married in 1969. And we're still together.

I met Jan at a dance in Bendigo, I think it was in May 1965. The boys went around and asked the girls for a dance, and one of the earliest conversations we both recall is when I asked her where she was from. She said, 'Oh, you wouldn't know where it is.'

I said, 'Why don't you tell me? I might.'

She said, 'Sea Lake.'

That's the next big town down from Ouyen, so I said, 'I know Sea Lake. Do you live near there?'

She said she did, so I named a small-town, Boigbeat. 'No. So you know those towns?' she asked.

'Yes,' I said. 'What about Berriwillock? Is that where you live?'

She said, 'Yes,' and that was the kind of impetus that got us going.

Jan was a student teacher at Bendigo Teachers' College at the time and was going away on school holidays. So I said, 'Well, we might meet up at the dance here again after the school holidays.' So we did.

We were married on 4 January 1969. I have to say, not in a crude sense at all, that as a male it was a dream. I had never thought about it, but I suppose as a male matures sexually and relationships-wise, the responsibility of marriage, and finding a house and beginning to buy furniture, and no doubt having talks about having children at some stage—those things develop in you. They're probably not real fast learning curves—courting the one girl for four years, even then that was sort of a slow process in the minds of maybe half the males of my cohort. But it was just ideal for both Jan and me.

1969
'OUR WEDDING DAY PHOTO'

Her parents were brilliantly respectful of me. And all I was doing was hitchhiking up to meet their daughter, sleeping out in a sleepout unsupervised by them. I was humbled by it. My mother was a micro-manager of my two older brothers' relationships. As the next in the family to start going-out to dances, I remember clearly thinking, *I'll bloody pick a girl that mum will really like.* Well, that didn't *effing* work, to the point—and this is part of my learning and growing up—I ended up where I couldn't mention her to my brothers and sisters without calling her *Mrs AW*, which is my dad's initials, not hers. I couldn't call her *Mum*, she so infected me with negative attitudes.

Going through teachers' college, towards the end of the year, you're asked, 'Here's a list of schools with vacancies for agriculture teachers. Put a preference down, with a minimum of three.'

On my Application to the Education Department I put a heading, *'Nowhere north of the Great Divide',* because my mum would be north of that Divide. Well, they didn't bloody take any notice of that. Here's Graham Trimble having to learn fast to step up to Bureaucracy. The schools that I had indicated were all south of the Divide.

I went into the Department and I said, 'You've allocated me to Echuca—that's north of the Divide.'

'Yes, we thought you'd best fit in up there,' was the official's response.

I said, 'I will best fit in below the Divide.' Anyway, I had it changed, and ended up teaching in Sale, Gippsland, for nine years. Our two daughters, Toni and Simone, were born there. Now that's a great learning experience.

Later I left teaching and went into selling insurance—another growing-up event, another monstrous experience.

It didn't take me long—and I'm talking about a few days at a training school with National Mutual—to realise the power there is in being reasonably well-dressed, with a tie and having a business card. I'd knock on an accountant's door and ask for an appointment, then straight away say, 'Now, I'm here to sell you insurance and talk about superannuation, either for yourself or your clients or your business. But if you don't want to talk about it, that's alright. I'm happy to pay for the appointment.'

'Oh, that's alright. Don't worry about it,' they would usually say.

I felt there was a power, in that maybe 95% of the population don't understand insurance, and don't understand financial planning. They don't want to engage in those kinds of risk-averse topics. It got to the point after just a year and a half in insurance, that a Fire and General guy rang me up and said, 'I've got a guy who's a shop steward with one of the offshore oil/gas platforms in Bass Strait, and they want to have a talk about superannuation.'

I said, 'Yeh, sure.' And Geoff, representing three very powerful unions, came along. I knew only to have a blank sheet of paper on the table and a pen. Don't have anything else—don't have pens in your pockets, don't have folders, don't have books, don't look like an insurance guy, even though you are. On the piece of paper, probably foolscap size, write a big 1, 2, 3, 4. I said to Geoff: 'What do you and your members want?' And they listed them out. Within a year and a half, I had instigated and helped negotiate with these union guys the largest superannuation scheme negotiated by a single insurance agent in National Mutual's and T&G's history. My first cheque from that deal, $26,000, was virtually the same as my final year's teaching salary.

Offcuts 3

What a dream-run of events I have had and I'm still expecting to grow, from here on. Just to further reflect—the experiences and relationships I have gained by being a member of the Oxley Men's Shed. *Wow!* What a great bunch of blokes to help me top up my manual skills and personal experiences. I still have some growing-up to do. Thank you.

David Hands

THE TEA TREE SCHOOL – A LESSON LEARNT

IN THE 1970S I WAS LIVING in Alice Springs and working with the Department of Works as Engineer for Services. In this job, I got to work on several water, power, and building projects throughout an area covering around 60% of the Northern Territory extending from the Queensland border across to Giles in Western Australia, and as far north as Borroloola on the Gulf.

I got to meet and work with many people who had lived for most of their lives in the Territory. One of these named Bill was born at a cattle property out on the Barclay Highway near Avon Downs in the early 1920s. He was taught to read by the station manager's wife and had no formal education, but a strong thirst for knowledge. There were many people living in remote areas of Australia at that time who had little or no education.

During World War II, Bill worked with the Allied Work Force, building the road from the rail head at Mt Isa up to Darwin, and after the war, had the General Store and newsagency in Tennant Creek. He lived there for more than 10 years and became a JP.

In the mid 1960s he moved to Alice Springs and worked with the Department of Works, heading up the Registry section. He was one of the most knowledgeable people I had met.

OFFCUTS 3

I had been working at Mereenie, south of Alice Springs, and when I returned to the office, Bill had an enormous grin on his face after receiving the weekly set of tender documents from Darwin. He said, 'Have a look at the school they are planning to build at Tea Tree. Do they know where Tea Tree is?'

The design of the school bore a strong resemblance to those recently built in Alice Springs and Tennant Creek to accommodate 160 to 200 students. It had ducted heating and cooling, with oil-fired boilers, large central air-handling units, a kitchen and dining area.

'Have they got confused with Tea Tree north of Adelaide?' he asked.

Tea Tree in the NT is about 190 km north of Alice on the Stuart Highway. It had a roadhouse, a police station and a small trailer school with about 11 students. The official population was 70, including nearby cattle stations. However the actual population was about 25. There was no town power or water available in Tea Tree, with only a small bore serving the roadhouse and police station. The bore water was very sweet-tasting and did not meet WHO Standards.

Bill knew a lot of people in the Territory, and he went away to find someone we could talk to. A few days later, he came back with the name of a person in Canberra. 'One of the wise men in the East,' he called them.

We spoke with him, and it became clear that he did not know where Tea Tree was, but he promised to investigate it and get back to us. Nothing more was heard, until about six weeks later. A press release was issued and a contract was awarded to build the

Tea Tree School, NT

school. I later learned that you do not stand in the way of a public servant who is trying to commit money by June 30.

The school was duly completed the following year and, as there was still no power or water available, it was unable to be used so it was fenced and locked up. A few months later, a press release was issued stating that the school would be opened by the Federal Minister for Education after Parliament rose for the year at the end of November.

We suggested that this may not be a good idea as temperatures were likely to be over 40°C and, without power and water, the cooling could not be operated, and the toilets could not be flushed.

At the time, Water Resources had a drilling rig returning from up at the Gulf, and whilst the chances of finding good quality water was low, it was decided they would stop over at Tea Tree and sink a bore at the rear of the school. Things at first looked promising with water being found at a depth of about 8 metres. However, the sample analysis indicated that the bore had been drilled through a runoff trench from the septic tank at the police station next door.

OFFCUTS 3

The borehole was quickly sealed.

We were then directed to construct a 45,000-litre water storage tank and pressure pump along with a temporary generator to provide power for the official opening. I quoted a price that I thought would deter them, but shortly afterwards received an order to proceed.

The job was completed in time for the official opening and filled with water trucked in from Aileron, about 80 km to the south.

The Minister for Education arrived for the opening and, after a walk around the site, quickly worked out what had happened and realised that the school could not be used in the near future. He was not impressed and was heard to say on the return drive back to Alice Springs that he would 'remove the manhood of the person responsible.'

The official response from the Education Department was that 'the person responsible could not be found, that valuable

lessons had been learnt and procedures revised to ensure that such a thing would never happen again.' A response worthy of Sir Humphrey Appleby in *Yes, Minister* and one that I have heard many times since then.

The go-ahead was given early the following year to provide a permanent water supply to Tea Tree from a bore field around 5 km south of the town and to provide water storage and fire pumps in the town. The work was completed about six months later.

On one of our regular trips up the Stuart Highway to Tennant Creek we saw that construction work was underway on a power station to the northwest of Tea Tree. We also saw construction work going on a few hundred metres south which we assumed was housing being built for the local Aboriginal Housing Corporation. Similar work was taking place at the time in other remote townships in Central Australia.

On our return trip back to Alice Springs, we called into the site. The foreman told us that the project was for several houses, and it also included a power station.

Peter Darmody

On our return to Alice Springs, we followed this up with the relevant authorities, one of whom asked: 'Is Tea Tree the same place as Ti Tree?' The second power station building was completed and used as a storage shed.

The school began operating the following year with 16 students along with 11 teaching and support staff.

I left Alice Springs in 1978 after the Northern Territory was given self-government, since my work was divided up between the NT and the Commonwealth. I had expected to remain in Alice Springs for many years more and had owned a house there.

I was given the option of moving to Darwin or to Canberra. I chose Canberra.

In 1983, the name of Tea Tree was officially changed to Ti Tree.

In 2019, the official population of Ti Tree had risen to 88. The school continues to operate.

GOING TROPPO IN TONGA

In the 1980s, I went to Vava'u in the Kingdom of Tonga to commission a new hospital, a bulk fuel storage depot, and a ship-to-shore pipeline being built as part of Australian Aid to Tonga. Other Australian Aid projects at that time included a wharf in the harbour and a power station at Ha'apai.

The trip from Australia took three days with stopovers in Auckland and Nukualofa. The final leg to Vava'u was on a 12-passenger Twin Otter aircraft.

When I was in Nukualofa, I called into the Australian Embassy for a briefing and was then taken to the Tongan Ministry of Works, a short distance away, for a meeting with the Department Secretary. He told me that tenders were still being reviewed and suggested that if I had time, I should visit the BP fuel depot on the foreshore. He gave me the name of the manager.

The following morning, I went to the depot, introduced myself and told the manager that I was going up to Vava'u to commission the fuel tank depot. I told him that I would see him up there if they won the tender to operate the facility.

Peter Darmody

He said, 'What do you mean, "If we get it"? For what we have paid that bastard, we had better get the contract.'

I replied, 'Okay, I'll see you up there next week.'

Vava'u has a beautiful deepwater harbour, Port of Prince, and at the time, a grass airstrip. Before landing, we flew a low pass over the strip to scare off the wild pigs. I was met by our building supervisor Glen who had been on Vava'u since the work began. I was taken to the hotel I would be staying at and, as we had a couple of drinks together, Glen filled me in on the two projects.

The hotel was located on a hill overlooking Neiafu with magnificent views of the harbour. It was built by an Australian developer but, due to the small number of tourists, was losing money and falling into disrepair.

Glen was a registered builder with more than 20 years' experience working on a wide range of projects, including hospitals in regional and western NSW. His children had grown up and left home. His wife had recently completed training as a midwife, and both were looking forward to working in developing countries. Glen had good people skills and an attitude of 'get the job done first and sort out the paperwork later'—attributes that are valuable when working in remote areas and developing countries.

Communication with Vava'u was by a HF radio link to Nukualofa where it could be connected to the international phone system. Installed by the American military in World War II, the link was frequently failing and was adversely affected by bad weather.

The following morning, I went up to the hospital site with Glen and did an initial inspection of the building services and medical gases. The design of the hospital was similar to medical facilities built in remote areas in the NT that I had previously worked on. It included two operating rooms, recovery areas, general wards, consulting rooms and a dental suite.

Having regard to the location and the limited local resources, the design was kept simple, used factory-built units wherever possible and included redundant equipment for key areas. A standby generator was provided.

Peter Darmody

Water for the hospital came from a bore up the hill behind the hospital that supplied water to a 45-kilolitre storage tank on a 15-metre tankstand.

The hospital was ready for commissioning. I planned to do the necessary testing over the next two weeks. A specialist technician was coming from Sydney the following week to commission the dental chairs.

The following day I went to the bulk fuel storage depot. There were three horizontal tanks, two larger vertical tanks, a tank refilling facility and fuel transfer pumps. A pipeline ran down the cliff face and out to a tanker mooring point in the bay.

Up until this facility was built, fuel was supplied to Vava'u from Nukualofa in 44-gallon drums on the fortnightly barge, a former US military landing vessel. This service was irregular due to the age of the vessel, the frequent need for maintenance and the availability of a paying load.

Offcuts 3

Anthony Durrington

The bulk fuel depot was being built by a specialist contractor from Newcastle with extensive experience in fuel-handling installations.

From my initial inspection of the site, I could see that the installation was substantially complete, was built to a high standard and appeared to be ready for testing.

I had arranged to meet with the contractor's workers on site to go through the commissioning plan. They arrived mid-morning, having had a heavy bout of drinking the night before. I soon discovered that this was a regular occurrence. They told me that their foreman had sold a lot of the company's tools and equipment, had shot through and was believed to be somewhere in New Zealand. Police had been notified.

Consequently, they were not able to do the normal testing that I had planned to undertake.

The tanks had all been filled with water and there were no leaks evident.

Glen and I made a manometer using some clear plastic tube, conduit saddles and a piece of chipboard. We went to the local Tongan Works Department depot, an old Nissen hut built by the US military in World War II, where we found an old bore column coupling on the scrapheap at the back. We were able to cut this in half using an old power hacksaw taken from Germany as reparation after the end of World War I, braze a plate onto each piece, and fit a truck tyre valve.

A hand-operated tyre pump was used to pressure test the larger vertical tanks. A length of galvanised water pipe with a paint tin brazed on the end was used to test the horizontal tanks. These were our improvised testing equipment.

The testing Standard required that the larger vertical tanks be pressurised to 2.5 kPa to test the integrity of the top weld. I handed the improvised testing equipment to the contractor, told him to pump the tank up to the line that I marked on the chipboard, and hold it there for one hour.

I went to the hospital and returned four hours later. I found that the contractor had organised a group of local men to do the pumping and was paying them 10 cents for each 10-minute shift. Six large Tongan men lined up on the roof of the tank was a sight to remember.

When I asked them how they went, they told me that they could only get the tank pressure up to half that required and that the pressure dropped when they stopped pumping. I quickly discovered that most of the fittings on the roof of the tank had been installed without gaskets at the flanges. I taped up the flanges and arranged for a retest to be done. The tank passed, and the other tanks were tested the following day and also passed.

Upon checking the drawings, I noted that many of the valves had been fitted to the wrong flanges. They told me that this was done hastily when they found out that the King of Tonga was coming up from Nukualofa the next day to officially open the facility.

Pressure testing of the pipeline from the harbour was a more straightforward exercise. A few of the rubber ring joints were leaking. This can often be fixed by loosening the Victaulic joint and rotating the coupling. If this does not work, the rings are usually replaced. Two joints required replacement.

During this process, it was discovered that the rings installed were for use on water pipes and not suitable for fuel oil products. The correct rings had been sent to the site and were found in an unopened crate at the rear of the site shed.

Installing the correct rings and retesting was expected to take up to three weeks. I called off the visit by the BP manager and prepared a defects list for Glen to action, as I would be returning to Australia.

This project reinforced the lessons I had learned from working on projects in remote areas in the NT, namely: pick your people carefully, rotate them on a regular basis, communicate regularly.

Wikistopher, CC BY-SA 4.0
creativecommons.org

Commissioning of the services at the hospital proceeded without any major problems found. The dental suction system required some replacement parts from Australia. These had been ordered and the local plumber instructed on how to install them.

Before leaving Vava'u, I met the doctor who would be running the hospital. His salary and that of many of his supporting staff was being paid by the Mormon Church.

His response was, 'That's okay. Before this hospital was built, if people on Vava'u became seriously ill or were injured in an accident, unless they could afford to get to Nukualofa, they often died.'

It made me appreciate how fortunate I was to be living in Australia.

Tonga is a poor country and is heavily dependent on aid from other countries, churches, and organisations such as the World Bank and UNICEF. Since I was there, the hospital has been extended several times, Vava'u has been linked to the international phone system, and the airport now has a sealed runway able to take 72-seat aircraft. More hotels have been built and cruise ships regularly visit the port.

JEFF THORPE

TEA OR COFFEE?

'TIS A TOPIC ABOUT which many ruminate
to try to find the trigger which makes us urinate.
Tea and coffee are prime suspects 'cos they contain caffeine,
yet this is fabrication, if you know what I mean.
Regular tea and coffee drinkers suffer no diuretic effect,
but occasional slurpers, with the toilet may connect,
theirs only a brief reaction to an unaccustomed brew,
the body soon adjusts to a sudden caffeine coup.

I digress, this tale is not about when or not we pee,
more to tell the story of the staple coffee and tea.
Where to start, their history knows no bounds
both of these beverages having outstanding backgrounds,
each are known worldwide as a satisfying drink
from tinged with milk and sugar to black as newsprint ink,
their origins steeped in legend, folklore of long ago
that only fuels their aura even more so.

Peter Darmody

Offcuts 3

The mythical story of tea began in China, 2737 BC
when Emperor Shen Hung sat beneath a tree
as his servant boiled water for drinking.
By chance, leaves fell to the water, sinking
infusing flavour to the liquid, pleasing Shen's taste
a quirk of fate surely not misplaced
for tea was born of the leaf of *Camellia Sinensus*,
a brew of choice preference by overwhelming consensus.

Legend or not, China led the world in tea consumption
centuries before the west by best assumption,
Japan was next to savour tea's flavours
Buddhist monks who learnt in China the prime conveyors,
green tea especially, the monks' favourite brew,
hence, tea drinking in Japan took not long to accrue.
The Dutch led Europe to tea with Chinese imports in 1606,
it became a trendy drink, adding more countries to the mix.

Anthony Durrington

As a nation of tea drinkers, Britain's acceptance was quite slow
till the British East India Company in 1664 started the flow.
Even then, tea was too expensive for many due to tax
introduced in 1689, 'twas 1964 before all levies did relax.
The punitive tariff led to smuggling in the eighteenth century
until William Pitt the Younger, in a Bill parliamentary
severely slashed the tax in 1784,
making tea affordable, banishing smuggling evermore.

Coffee, by comparison, has not the longevity of tea
although it too is touched by legend in its pedigree,
starting with a tale from the Ethiopian plateau
about goat herder Kaldi whose beasts grew to know
berries from a certain tree made them energetic,
this obvious to their master and not just theoretic.
Kaldi told a local Abbott who mixed the berries in a drink,
discovering the beverage and alertness had a definite link.

Anthony Durrington

Offcuts 3

In truth, Yemen in Arabia saw the first coffee cultivation.
From the fifteenth century the drink reached commendation
from thousands of pilgrims travelling to Mecca each year
the 'Wine of Araby' seen as a drink held dear.
Reaching Europe by the sixteen hundreds though not
    without dispute,
some called coffee, 'The Bitter Invention of Satan', vile
    potion absolute
yet, Pope Clement VIII as arbiter, invited to intervene,
sampled and liked the brew, approving the coffee bean.

In mid-seventeenth century coffee reached New York
but the footing of British tea proved hard to uncork.
But in 1773 the Boston Tea Party rose against tea's tax
and, as preferred American drink, it quickly got the axe.
American President Jefferson helped tea's status come unfurled,
stating 'Coffee—the favourite drink of the civilised world'.
Americans are arguably now the world's greatest coffee drinkers
adopting this patriotic stance 'hook, line and sinkers'.

An instance of coffee's standing being no oddity
is that after crude oil it's the world's most sought commodity;
and try to stand between Britons and their tea
is a task I'd set for you rather than for me.
Black or white, sweetened or not, either drink is fine
from pots or bags or percolators, drinkers stand in line
to have a relaxing 'cuppa' and invariably, a chat,
all things being equal, there's nothing wrong with that.

JIM PASCOE

A NIGHT AT THE OPERA

I HAVE LISTENED to all kinds of music and enjoyed most of it, although the heavy metal and hard rock don't give me much joy. My dad played in the Windsor Municipal Band while growing up and also learned the piano from his mother.

I have never played a musical instrument but have always enjoyed a good old singsong.

It came to pass that on my travels to Dalveen, I would eventually find the love of my life, Janice, who lived in Warwick. She and her sister Vona were members of the Warwick Choral Society. Their practice hall was situated down by the Condamine River not far from where they lived and a fair distance from any habitation.

Their group consisted of quite a large group of singers with most of them being their age or in their early twenties. Each year, the society held a performance of an operetta in the Warwick City Hall. There were very good productions with *Miss Hook of Holland, Salad Days* and *The Boyfriend* being some of them. *The Boyfriend* was a memorable one for me as I was tasked with the purchase of an item of ladies underwear called 'Witches Britches'. This underwear consists of frilly long knickers and, when worn, are shown below the hem of short skirts.

These items were unobtainable in the Warwick shops, and Janice asked me if I could look around Brisbane for a pair for her to wear. As I was working in Fortitude Valley at the time, I walked down to McWhirters Emporium at lunchtime and, lo and behold, on enquiring, found that this particular item was obtainable in the Ladies Wear department.

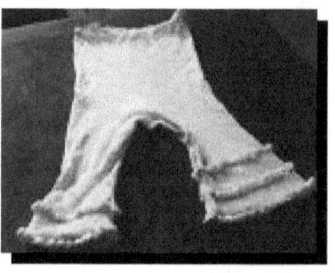

1960s Witches Britches. Image from sportslinkup.

I must say that I was a slightly embarrassed twenty-year-old when buying this item but blustered my way through by saying that they were a birthday present for my wife. I then received some enquiring looks from the sales staff as I walked out of the store with the item in question firmly tucked under my arm.

I presented this package to Janice when I arrived at her house on the next Friday night and she was 'over the moon'. At the Saturday afternoon practice, she showed all the other girls in the cast just what I had been able to obtain for her in Brisbane.

Needless to say, I came home to Brisbane with orders for various sizes of another ten 'Witches Britches'. The look that I received from the female sales staff at McWhirters the next day was something different.

Ten more sets of various sized 'Witches Britches' for my wife? I hoped that they didn't think that I was a cross-dresser, and so I had to honestly tell them why they were really required. Exit a red-faced Jim but with all the required underwear.

This show was a success and the costumes unbelievable to say the least.

One other item that the Choral Society participated in were the eisteddfods that were held in the surrounding towns—namely Brisbane, Stanthorpe and also Toowoomba. The one held at the Toowoomba City Hall was well-attended. The only trouble was that it rained all the way from Warwick and on the return trip, the rain became heavier. It is not a nice experience driving on a rainy blacksoil-covered bitumen road.

Peter Darmody

The most memorable eisteddfod that I attended with Janice was held in the Brisbane City Hall. Choral societies attended from all over the state. It was held over the 1965 Easter weekend and Janice and her sister stayed at her aunt's house in Bardon. The choir had their recital on the Saturday night and their practice was held at the community hall in Paddington. There were also single vocal recitals as well and Janice was a contestant in one of these, which was held on the Saturday afternoon. She was contestant number thirteen, followed by another twenty-seven singers. The song to be adjudicated upon was *I Love The Merry Minstrels That Come To My Garden.*

Peter Darmody

To cut a long story short, I enjoyed some of those that sang before Janice and certainly her solo. I had to, didn't I? However, I thought that the rest would never finish. Having heard that song sung forty times in a row, I must admit that it was now embedded into my brain. Since that day, *The Merry Minstrels* is not one of the tunes that I now sing very often. The things that you do for love.

Following the finalisation of the eisteddfod and the prizes being awarded, we travelled to the Avro Theatre at Bulimba to see *The Patsy,* starring Jerry Lewis followed by *Tom Jones,* that raunchy movie starring Albert Finney and Dianne Cilento.

Janice and Vona's parents would never have permitted them to see that movie in Warwick. To top off that night, I returned home with chewing gum stuck to the seat of my new brown-striped stove-pipe trousers and with bed bug bites around my waistline. That's what you get when you sit in the canvas seats.

That was another very memorable occasion that we both had with the Warwick Choral Society, and we both have a good laugh at what happened over that weekend. Her parents never ever found out about the trip to the movies.

THE HOLIDAY THAT WASN'T

I served six years as a member of the Royal Australian Naval Reserve based at HMAS *Moreton* in New Farm. It was a requisite that Tuesday night meetings and weekend training sailing around Moreton Bay would be undertaken on a regular basis.

Another requirement was that a thirteen-day annual continuous training period would be carried out each year. These training periods could be carried out on any ship in the fleet or ashore at any naval establishment in Australia.

During my time in the Reserve, HMAS *Mildura*, an old Bathurst Class minesweeper, was used as a static training vessel, together with two forty-foot work boats and HMA *GPV 957*, an old war-time general purpose vessel that was the main craft used for training in Moreton Bay. Eventually she didn't pass survey and was decommissioned. We were then presented with a motor refrigerated lighter HMA *MRL253*, another World War II era vessel. This craft had previously been home ported at HMAS *Terangau,* Manus Island.

Peter Darmody

A fair amount of work was required before she was ready for sea, as a fire had broken out in her engine room which was extinguished by purposely being flooded. She was of steel construction and, compared to the previous wooden-hulled boat, was more seaworthy.

I spent two of my training periods on her whilst she was lying alongside HMAS *Moreton*, which enabled me to go home each night instead of having to sling a hammock.

These training courses were quite profitable for me as, being an electrical apprentice in the Brisbane City Council, Department of Electricity, and also a member of the electrical branch in the Reserves, I was paid not only by the navy but my employer. I didn't have to make up my apprentice time as I was carrying out electrical work. Double pay, you little beauty.

Being unable to undertake my scheduled training in 1963 on board HMAS *Anzac*, sailing to Darwin, due to being involved in a motor vehicle accident, it wasn't until 1964 that I attended training on board HMAS *Teal*, a Ton Class minesweeper, of which six were obtained from the United Kingdom in 1962.

These craft were of wooden-hulled construction and twin-screwed and were very wet and uncomfortable to be aboard during rough weather.

My most memorable training period was on board HMAS *Parramatta*, which was then classed as a type 12 frigate. Day One was spent travelling from South Brisbane Railway Station to Sydney on the Interstate Express. On arrival and reporting to the RTO (Rail Transport Office), I was informed that my ship was at sea and would be arriving in Jervis Bay next morning. I was given a rail pass to Nowra Bomaderry from where I was transported to HMAS *Cresswell*, the officer training establishment situated beside Jervis Bay.

Reporting in, I entered the mess for a meal, where I was met by the cook who was an old school mate from Corinda Primary School. He was an orphan and had lived at Blackheath Home in Oxley before joining the navy as a junior recruit when he finished school. He had had a very hard life.

Peter Darmody

Next morning after breakfast, at the ship's office I was informed that HMAS *Parramatta* had experienced a defect in her gunnery and had returned to Garden Island Naval Base in Sydney for the necessary repairs.

Being presented with new orders to return to Sydney by train with another sailor, we both were driven to HMAS *Albatross*, the naval air station nearby. On arrival we reported to the base regulating office and were issued with white gaiters and patrol belts and further orders to escort a deserter back to Sydney on the train. He too was a crew member of HMAS *Parramatta* and had been 'dobbed in' by his girlfriend. He had over-stayed his leave with her and gone to the red-light district in Kings Cross. Hell hath no fury like a woman scorned.

The train journey and company were quite enjoyable and, on arrival at Central Station in Sydney, the naval shore patrol were waiting for us. We all climbed into the rear of the paddy wagon for our trip to Garden Island and HMAS *Parramatta*.

Reporting to the ship's office on board, I was surprised to see that the ship's writer (who in civilian life would be classed as a secretary) was someone I knew when he was a railway porter at Indooroopilly Railway Station in Brisbane. This was Day Three of my training with ten to go.

As the ship had been to sea for some time, local leave was given and I was presented with a two-day pass which I gratefully accepted. Once ashore, I booked into Naval House (Johnnies) for the duration of my shore leave.

Returning on board, the ship eventually departed Sydney for a two-day cruise before returning to Garden Island. After a couple of days alongside, we took a short trip to moor off Manly, as HMAS *Parramatta* was selected to be the official ship at the Festival of the Pines Celebration. We received hundreds of visitors on board during the time that we were moored there.

Following this event, HMAS *Parramatta* was sailing to New Zealand for a goodwill visit and this caused a bit of a problem for me with the ship's office, as I would be overstaying my training, if continuing on board.

Peter Darmody

There were three options mooted regarding me. One was that I would be transferred by breeches buoy to another ship while at sea, or alternatively flown home when the ship reached New Zealand, or else having my training period signed off as finalised before sailing and then being sent home early.

The last eventually happened, and my final cruise was by a tug, towing a barge with the ship's mooring anchor, as my transport back to Garden Island, from where I was driven to Central Station and issued my rail ticket home.

So far, I had only completed ten days' training and, on arrival in Brisbane, decided to spend the rest of the time at my girlfriend's uncle's farm at Turners Creek, Dalveen. After dropping off my gear at home in Corinda, I decided to hitch-hike and save some money. The first pick-up was with a painter driving a Morris Minor utility loaded with paint tins. He was heading to St George to work on a property. On leaving Ipswich, he stopped at every hotel, where we had two beers, before eventually dropping me off at the Drayton turnoff on the western side of Toowoomba. I didn't have to wait long before a couple who were returning to Sydney from their honeymoon offered me a lift south.

On arrival in Warwick, the wife suggested a drink was needed and we pulled up at the Horse and Jockey Hotel for sustenance. After some time, we headed off as they were staying in Stanthorpe for the night and it was getting late.

It's twenty-five miles from Warwick to Turners Creek, Dalveen, and on arrival at the road turnoff, I asked him if he could drop me off there. Instead, he drove all the way down the road and dropped me at the front gate but didn't drive in as he wanted to get into town before dark.

My arrival was unexpected, but welcomed, as they were planting over three thousand cabbages the next day, and extra hands were always helpful and appreciated.

And that is where I completed my annual continuous training— with two lots of pay, received together with a certificate stating that thirteen days of electrical training had been carried out during that time. This paperwork was duly presented to the Electricity Department paymaster on my return to work and the pertinent details recorded into my apprenticeship papers.

How can I say that it was the 'holiday that wasn't' with four train trips, two cruises, a leave period and then finally a few days' rest in the Granite Belt, when in all honesty only a fraction of one of those thirteen-day training periods was part of my naval service?

WHO'S COUNTING?

Sitting in the sun on the balcony of my unit this winter's day, I considered myself lucky, as my son had just phoned me. He said that it was -3°C in Stanthorpe when he arrived back home after returning from Sydney with a 'B double' semi-trailer load of chocolates that was bound for Brisbane.

He's lucky that his home is only two kilometres from the Lindsay Brothers transport depot, as his old Toyota utility has no air-conditioning and, at three o'clock in the morning, the windscreen is iced over.

This reminded me of when, before our marriage, I used to stay at my wife's uncle's farm with her cousins Jim and Ross and also of the things we did in the winter time. Of course, rising at five-thirty in the morning and getting the milking cows in from the bottom paddock always came to the fore. How cold it could get in the dairy as the sun came up! Thank goodness for the porridge we always had before starting the milking.

We will say nothing about our overnight fishing trips to the creek where there was always a good fire and a bottle of Bundaberg

Rum to pass around. They both kept the cold at bay while waiting for the fish to bite.

Another activity that always occurred in winter was going armed with our kerosene tins into the cultivation and picking beans. It's amazing how many beans are attached to each bush, and you think that you are never going to finish the row.

The bean-picking exercise always seemed to occur when the weather decided that we couldn't have too much of a good thing and therefore it would bring in the sleet, accompanied by a sneaky breeze. Protection from the elements was required and so overalls, gum boots and of course the obligatory sugarbag headcover were donned before venturing out. (For the uninitiated: the sugarbag was inverted in half to keep your head and back sort of free from the dampness.)

Of course, when the beans were finally picked, they were bagged up in the farm shed which was much warmer. Auntie Una always made sure that we always had a hot cup of tea available for us. And then yes, it was time for the afternoon milking and here we go again.

The next-door neighbour, who I will call Jack, never went into vegetables and only worked with sheep, although he had a milking cow for his home use. He had a five-hundred-acre property there and another property consisting of two, two-hundred-acre paddocks about ten miles away down the Cunningham Highway towards Warwick. He called this place *Mountside*.

A dirt road off the highway took us to these paddocks and the only improvements to them were a race and a small set of yards for enclosing livestock. These yards and race always reminded me

Offcuts 3

Peter Darmody

of the *Saltbush Bill* comics as they were pretty well run-down. There were Cobb and Co wire ties everywhere that were holding up the rails of the race and yards and the gate was held up with bailing twine.

One cold winter's day, Jack came over to the farm and asked cousins Jim, Ross and myself if we could come down to *Mountside* and help muster one of these paddocks as his two hundred sheep there needed to be drenched and tagged. He would meet us down there after he picked up the drenching gun and drench from home.

On arrival at *Mountside*, we waited for Jack to arrive and there was no shelter available for protection from a very sneaky little breeze that began to blow over the hills. Jack finally arrived in his old World War II Jeep with

Brian Goeldner

all the necessary equipment, together with a couple of dogs, and we then set off to muster this paddock.

The paddock here was one of the roughest paddocks that I have ever mustered. It consisted of heavily scrubbed trap rock country and very steep hilly ground so that mustering could only be carried out on horseback or, in our case, on foot.

Jack was waiting down on the flat in his Jeep and would muster the sheep into the yards with his dogs when we brought them down. The sheep in question were four-tooth cross-bred Merino wethers and were bred in the Walgett area. They were very large sheep and very wild.

Paul Watkins

The muster began with us climbing up into the hills and slowly gathering up the sheep and bringing them down to meet Jack and the dogs. Now Jack had a tally of 200 as the number of sheep supposedly in this paddock and, unfortunately, this number didn't match up with what we had brought down. We had gathered up only one hundred and seventy head.

So it was another trip up into the hills and, by now, it had begun to sleet and was becoming very uncomfortable. The grass was knee-high and our legs were wet but, having brought wet weather gear with us, we remained relatively dry. This muster brought down another twenty-five sheep and Jack said that another muster of the paddock should do it. So, once again, we climbed the hills and prodded into every gully and rock and eventually brought down another thirty wethers and one ewe.

Yes, you may say one hundred and seventy plus twenty-five plus thirty equals two hundred and twenty-five, although there were only supposed to be two hundred sheep in this paddock. Jack's tally count never added up. At least we had all the sheep in the yards and we now began to drench and tag them so that we could get back to a warm home again.

To add to our misery, while driving his Jeep, Jack drove over a log that flicked up and hit him across his nose and took a slice of skin off. He left to drive to the Warwick Base Hospital for treatment, leaving us to complete the drenching and tagging.

Mustering is complete.

This job was done in a relatively short time as we had two drench guns in operation, with one of us working from either end of the race while the third yarded the sheep. He had more trouble than us as, due to the condition of the yards, some of the sheep jumped over the sides. He was kept quite busy.

With the drenching and tagging completed and the number of sheep correctly added to the tally book, we waited for Jack to return. He arrived back with a large dressing applied across his nose and his eyes running with tears due to being unable to wear his glasses.

Tagging the sheep

'That was a great job that you did, boys,' he said. 'Let's go home and I'll shout you all a rum.'

Now this was a real highlight as Jack was not one who 'pushed the boat out' very often. Arriving at his house, and looking forward to this golden beverage, Jack sat us down around the kitchen table with the combustion stove warming us all up. We waited anxiously with bated breath for our well-earned reward as Jack left to make our drinks that we were sure would warm us up internally as well. After working in the sleet on a cold winter's day, a rum is certainly something to look forward to.

Yes, in he came with that tray of shimmering glasses of golden liquid. Having passed them around to all of us, Jack raised his glass and said, 'Here's cheers, boys, and thanks for today and a job well done. I couldn't have done it without you.'

We raised our glasses in return and took our first sip of this precious nectar, but something was wrong. That long-awaited drink tasted different. *What had Jack done?* Then it slowly dawned on us. He had adulterated this most precious commodity with water, yes, water.

This was a sacrilegious act to us discerning rum drinkers, and disappointment must have shown on all our faces to have received a reward of a watered-down rum for a full day of mustering on such a cold winter's day.

Jack was completely unaware of what he had done to us all, and we didn't let on and quickly finished our drinks before returning home.

That event occurred in 1964, sixty years ago and I've never forgotten it. Jack and Ross have been long gone and so, when Jim

Anthony Durrington

and I get together, especially at Easter time, we always propose a toast and drink to Jack and his rum-and-water toddy all those years ago.

By the way, since that time, a drink of rum and water has never again passed my lips.

James Vernon

FORE!

BEING RAISED IN my parents' boarding house gave me a range of experiences that contributed to my appreciation of people and life. Bert Schafferius (I hope that is spelt correctly) had an indirect influence on me. I first met him early one morning as I made the early morning walk to the backyard dunny. He was practising his golf swing with a hollow plastic ball that had quite large holes around its surface. It left the tee just like a real ball but wouldn't travel far and could do neither harm nor damage. 'Are you scaring the worms?' I asked rather cheekily. He laughed. In my book, any adult who could laugh at a kid's cheek (especially mine) had to be okay, so we became quite friendly.

Bert worked for the railways and was a 'confirmed bachelor', although on one occasion he did say that he intended marrying a twenty-year-old and trading her in for two more twenty-year-olds when she turned forty. But, most importantly, Bert played golf. When I became interested in it, one of the other boarders sold me an ancient set of golf clubs on a flexible time-payment plan. He suggested that the payment would start at a penny a week and double each week. A little mental arithmetic told me that that wasn't a particularly wise arrangement. We negotiated the terms to a more favourable two shillings a week. He generously waived the remainder of the debt when he left the house.

Well, with Bert's sponsorship, my clubs and my weekly income from the *Telegraph* newspaper, I became a junior member of Gailes Golf Club, conveniently situated on the doorstep of Gailes railway station. I signed up for lessons with the club's Pro, Arch McArthur. The day for my first lesson arrived. I had cleaned my clubs and polished the bag as well as possible. (This wasn't an easy task. They resembled neglected farm tools more than sporting equipment.) I set out with a jaunty step, hope in my heart and my pride and joy bouncing importantly against my back.

At the club I met the Professional. He was a dour Scot of indeterminate age who had the appearance of an animated garden gnome. When we reached the practice tee, he said, 'Put your clubs over there. We'll use this one.' With that he handed me a short, heavy club that looked even older than himself. 'It's a number one wood. Short shaft and large heavy head. It's the best club to learn with.' Then he laid out a line of tees and put a ball on each one. Naturally, I stepped up to the first ball.

Graham Murphy

'Not yet. You have to learn to swing the club first. We'll start with the grip and the stance. Like this. That's good. Now you imitate a pendulum. Take the club back to shoulder height and swing through to the same height on the other side.' I did so as he recited his mantra: 'Feel the weight of the club. Feel the weight of the head. Keep your head down. Feel the weight of the head. Keep your head down.'

What was this all about? I wanted to swing the club right back, à la Arnold Palmer, then swing down and around with sufficient force to smash an elephant's skull. (A metaphorical elephant, of course.)

'Keep your head down … feel the weight of the head …' and on and on until, 'That's okay. Now step up to the ball. Keep your head down and your eye on the ball. Now take the club back to shoulder height and swing it smoothly to the ball and follow through to the other shoulder.'

I did that. I missed the ball.

'Keep your head down and keep your eye on the ball. Try again.'

I did it again. This time the breeze from the club going past the ball dislodged it from the tee.

'Keep your head down and keep your eye on the ball. Try again.'

I tried again. I sliced. 'Remember the procedure. Try again.'

I hooked. I skyed the ball. I missed the ball. Every attempt led to a patient repetition from the slight Scottish accent.

'Keep your head down.'

'Keep your eye on the ball.'

'Follow through to the other shoulder. Try again.'

Finally, I hit the ball with a resounding THWACK. The gnome ducked as a large divot flew past his head. The real target flew up into the air and landed at least three metres behind me. When I turned to retrieve it, humiliation was added to frustration when I noticed a group on the verandah of 'the nineteenth hole' enjoying my agony as they indulged in the traditional post-game beer.

'Let's try again. What do you have to do?'

I dutifully repeated his mantra of instructions.

'Good. Come up to the ball, repeat them to yourself and then do it.'

I did as he instructed. The ball lifted gracefully into the air and came to rest a good thirty metres straight ahead in the centre of the fairway. 'Well done! That was a great shot! It was one of the best I've seen a boy do in his first lesson! Well done!'

'It was a fluke,' I grumped.

His voice changed. 'No, it wasn't. There is no such thing as a fluke in golf. YOU gripped the club correctly. YOU had the right stance. YOU kept your head down. YOU swung the club correctly and followed through. Now do it again.'

Peter Darmody

I moved along the line of tees. I hooked. I sliced. I skyed the ball. In a calm, gentle voice he said, 'I know what you were thinking. You were thinking of the number of times you were unsuccessful.'

I nodded sheepishly.

'Well, forget them. They aren't important. Think ONLY of the time it went straight down the fairway. When you are addressing the ball, remember how you felt then. Remember how it left your club and where it landed. Now, take your time and do it again. Think only of the successful shot. Take your time.'

I did as I was told. The ball landed in almost the same place. The next one went a little further. Then I missed the ball. 'Forget that one. Think of the successful shots. Think of what you did and how you felt on the successful times.'

I did.

'Great shot,' he exclaimed enthusiastically.

I found that the eighteen shillings a week that I earned from my Saturday afternoon job collecting sporting results for the Telegraph newspaper wouldn't stretch to golf lessons *and* cigarettes. I had a few games and could have been proud of my scores if I had been playing cricket.

However, the money I spent on the few lessons I did have was the best investment I could have made in my education. I recounted that story to under-achieving students many times in my teaching

Anthony Durrington

career with good effect. It's amazing how the impact of apparently inconsequential events lives on.

MAZEPA RIDES AGAIN[2]

We shouted ourselves and our two kids a couple of nights at a fairly luxurious resort in the Gold Coast hinterland. When we had unpacked, I looked through the brochure listing the resort's facilities and saw that horse-riding was available for all skill levels of horsemanship. What red-blooded father could resist the opportunity to take his first-born on an equine experience—a first time for both of them? I contacted the office immediately to make a booking. Naturally I informed the receptionist that we were both novices to saddles.

Early next morning we arrived at the meeting spot. At the appointed time a slip of a girl leading three horses appeared. The horses made an interesting contrast. There was a little pony, no doubt for my son. Then a medium-sized horse which I guessed was mine. Third was a gargantuan monster. That had to be for the instructor.

---

2   Ivan Mazepa (1639–1709) figures in Ukrainian, Russian and Polish history. His youthful inappropriate liaison with a Polish countess caused her husband to tie him on the back of a wild stallion and send him into the wilderness never to return. Mazepa foiled this plan by managing to free himself. Several artists of the romantic era celebrated his wild ride in their works. Lord Byron wrote a very long narrative poem about his equine adventure. A sanitised version was included in one of my primary school English texts.

She turned to my son and, as she was getting him on board, she asked, 'Can you mount yourself?' Well, I'd had a very good education in the processes of riding through all of those cowboy movies I had seen as a child, so I responded, 'Yeah, sure,' and turned to the middle horse.

Paul Watkins

'Not that one. You take the other horse. His name's Sergeant-major.' I gasped quietly and followed her direction.

I'm not the most agile person. The stirrup was so high off the ground I struggled to reach it. When I was halfway up, the horse turned his head to me and sneered. When I was finally in the saddle my feet couldn't reach the stirrups. I was so high in the air I decided not to look down. My attentive instructor noticed my predicament with the stirrups and adjusted them for me. As soon as I was settled my mount started walking of his own accord. 'Don't worry. He's just going for a drink before we leave,' the lass assured me. Sure enough, he ambled to the trough that ran the length of the barn wall and lowered his head to drink. His neck was so long that my hand not only went to the very end of the reins, but I had to lean forward slightly to retain my grip.

At the time I was a heavy smoker and had been since preteen years. In common with a lot of long-term nicotine addicts, I frequently had to clear my throat with a little cough. And that's what I did.

Sergeant-major reared up on his hind legs, did a u-turn in reverse and started careering around the corral.

Hopalong Cassidy had taught me that you stop a horse by sharply pulling back on the reins and yelling 'Whoa!' The only problem was that because of the position of the reins in my hand, they would have had to go back well past my ear. I did manage a loud 'Whoa!' but onlookers might have thought it sounded more like 'Oh, shit!'

There I was. My right hand was trying to yank the reins past the back of my head; my left hand was clutching the saddle so tightly that my knuckles could easily have burst through their confining skin and my camera was bouncing against my chest. All I could see was a brown, green and blue blur as the scenery, and possibly my life, flashed past me.

Peter Darmody

Then I was thrown forward so that my chest hit the back of his neck. Sergeant-major had screeched to a halt with his nose only inches from the wall of the barn. His head turned and he transfixed me with a look of pure evil.

The Junior Mistress of the Horses came over quickly, looked up at me with amazement smeared across her youthful face and said, 'You stayed on!'

What was I supposed to do? Fall off? You could break your neck falling off this horse when he was standing still.

'Do you want to get off?' she asked rather unnecessarily. I was about to answer in a very definite affirmative when I saw my son looking at me. His eyes bulged; his mouth was agape. I read his mind. *Is my horse going to do that?* I decided that I might restore his confidence if I remained in the saddle.

Sergeant-major continued to turn his head to stare at me. The look in his eyes progressed rapidly from evil to positively satanic.

'I think I will get off now,' I mumbled, and slid dangerously from the saddle to the inviting ground. 'He certainly is a big horse. Just how big is he?'

'He's a little over seventeen hands,' she responded innocently, and added, 'We've only had him for a few days. He was a trotter so he has a very smooth gait. That would be why you stayed on. He probably isn't used to a saddle.'

'You mean that I might be the first person to ride him.'

'Er, yes', came the slightly embarrassed reply.

Then the thought struck me that I had missed a golden opportunity. If I had come off him

Anthony Durrington

and broken my neck I could have sued the resort for a large payout and lived in financial security for the rest of my life. But I realised quickly that then I wouldn't be able to have any more kids. The world would have been deprived of the addition of two marvellous people.

Well, would I be silly enough to mount another horse after my encounter with that bearer of Bill the Bastard's genes?[3] Probably. Maybe there's a nice, quiet, geriatric Shetland pony waiting for me somewhere.

GUN SHY

School days finally dragged into time's rubbish bin. After a couple of weeks it dawned on me that it was time to get serious and look for a job. Dismal Senior results categorised me as being unsuitable for tertiary study. It wasn't until universities introduced mature age entry that I finally enrolled in a university as a counterbalance to the stresses of business. Then I learned that I wasn't the academic incompetent that my high school teachers had led me to believe I was. I was actually very academically competent.

I found that employers paid a lot of attention to school results. However, the Commonwealth Public Service had their own test to determine recruitment. Not long after the test I found myself in the Public Service Inspector's office where I was told that the Postmaster General (now Telstra) urgently needed my services.

---

3   Bill the Bastard was a mount in the Australian Light Horse during the First World War. He earned his name because he would allow only one man to ride him. All others would be quickly dispatched to eat dirt.

When I arrived there I found that the urgent need was for someone to relieve another clerk for three weeks when he went on recreation leave. The position included acting as armed escort on a pay delivery every second week. (In those days wages were personally delivered in cash, not by direct debit to a bank account.)

The beginning of the first pay week brought a real 'shock, horror, gasp' moment. My boss' boss informed me that I was to be the escort on a pay 'car'. Therefore, I would have to see someone in Postal Investigations to learn how to use a Browning 9 mm semi-automatic pistol. *What?* I did NOT want that. Fast thinking was required. 'Don't you have to be 21 to get a pistol licence in Queensland? I'm only 18.'

That made him think and say, 'Oh. I'd better check that.' He came back after lunch with the results of his research. 'It's OK. On payday you are regarded as being temporarily seconded to the Federal Police. You can go to Postal Investigations for your instruction now.' He could obviously teach me a bit about the art of bullshit.

I found my instructor sitting at a desk with an array of two pistols, a number of magazines and a box of cartridges in front of him. My first instruction was that the pistol had to be loaded at all times. *What? Oh no!* The second instruction was confusing. 'When you are in public you must NOT take the pistol out of your pocket under ANY circumstances.'

'What if we are held up?'

'Just give them the money. We don't want anyone getting killed because of silly heroics.'

Offcuts 3

'So why do we have the pistol?'

'It's a deterrent. And you should always vary your route so that would-be thieves can't predict where you'll be, especially when you collect the money from the Reserve Bank.' That was good advice, except that both the bank and the post office were in Queen Street. The route could only be varied by means of a long detour. Welcome to the Public Service, mate!

He then introduced me to the pistol. 'It's a very safe pistol because it has three safety features. First there's the safety catch...' He indicated the rotating lug that engaged on the slide to make it inoperable. '... then there's the rear trigger in the butt. The gun requires equal force on both triggers that are at 180 degrees to each other. So, if a loaded-and-cocked weapon is dropped, it won't fire.'

Brian Douglas MOD, OGL v1.0OGL v1.0, via Wikimedia Commons

Then he put a loaded magazine into the butt, pulled back the slide, removed the magazine, pointed the gun at my head and tried unsuccessfully to pull the trigger. 'See, it won't fire without the magazine, even if there's a round in the breech. A lot of accidents happen because people forget about the round in the breech. This pistol is foolproof.'

He went on. 'Now, if anything goes wrong and it jams or has any problem, don't try to fix it. Put the safety catch on and bring it back to me. See that?' He indicated a hole in the wall. 'That happened when I was trying to unjam a pistol. The bullet went right through the wall and missed the typist on the other side by inches.' *Didn't he say that the Browning was foolproof?*

The relief position was very demanding. It involved collecting pay envelopes and large sheets of yellow paper with the details of allowances for employees from costing section. These were then cut into individual pay slips, sorted into alphabetical order and inserted into the pay envelopes. This was a demanding task that required detailed knowledge of the alphabet. The stress of getting each slip into its own envelope would shatter a less developed intellect. Once the relief period was finished, I had two days per fortnight of gainful, if unpleasant, employment. The other eight days saw me moved around the department as some sort of commodity that was surplus to requirements.

These occupations found me doing important tasks such as sorting through 35 mm negatives to determine what the subject was. It seemed that while the photographer could take a reasonably well-exposed picture and process it, he was unable to record where and when it was taken. My task was to use a magnifying loupe or enlarger to find clues such as 'Bulloomacanker telephone exchange' on the building. I applied myself assiduously to this task in the hope that I might actually do some photography. After a couple of weeks I gave up on that hope. I had identified as many buildings as I could, so I approached the photographer and told him the rest were unidentifiable and suggested a different activity. His response was that he really expected me to finish the job.

So, I spent several days pretending to be conscientiously carrying out his instructions, concocting identifications, making chains of paperclips and hiding behind filing cabinets. When I figured he had forgotten my request to move on, I used my initiative and made an executive decision. As soon as he was out of the office, I put the leftover negatives into a large paper bag and deposited them in a rubbish bin on my way home. Next morning I proudly announced that I had finished the task. Then I moved on to similarly boring jobs such as working a pedal-operated collating machine to assemble a large collection of vital multiple page documents.

When payday arrived, I set off with the pay clerk to the GPO to collect the pistol and the cheque. There we stood in line at the accountant's desk. I collected and signed for the pistol and the loaded magazine. The pay clerk collected the cheque, a suitcase for the cash and a breakup of the denominations required to fill the envelopes without hunting for change. Then to the bank with the weight of the pistol trying to remove my trousers.

On one hilarious occasion a newcomer who had missed the firearm indoctrination was assigned to the task of escort. After signing for the gun, he picked up the weapon and magazine, rammed the magazine into the butt, pulled the slide back, no doubt as he had seen in the movies, pointed the gun at the accountant's head and said, 'What do I do now?'

The accountant, a bull-necked, ruddy-complexioned fellow who seemed to overflow his chair, looked up, turned an even brighter shade of red when he realised his precarious position and made an athletic dive for shelter under his desk. A panicked, strangled gasp came from that position. 'Just put it down. Just put it down!'

The following pay day we were handed a sheet of instructions for the safe handling of pistols. New procedures were introduced to ensure that no more untrained escorts were handed a gun.

After the trip to the bank to cash the cheque, it was back to the first floor of the GPO, past the cashier's enclosed office and through the room full of typists and accounting machine operators, their desks set out like the desks in a traditional classroom. At the head of the room the accountant sat like a teacher supervising the class. Finally into the counting room, its entry secured by a door fitted with a Yale lock. Any intruder with larcenous intent would have to ask the accountant politely for the key.

The room's interior contained several desks large enough to accommodate the suitcase, the money laid out in piles, and the pay envelopes. A bar that ran the length of the desk was set underneath it. This bar provided occasional amusement. If a newcomer to the scene complained about the heat, he would be told to turn the air conditioner on.

'How do I do that?'

'See the bar you're resting your feet on? Just kick it up.'

When he did this, it set off an excruciatingly loud alarm bell over the cashier's head, followed by a roar of language from him that one did not use in front of young ladies. Eventually the key for the alarm would be found and the bell silenced. Counting then continued accompanied by mirth.

The task finished, the suitcases of bulging pay packets were left in the room overnight, protected by the lock on the door. The pistols were returned to the cashier.

Next day all the packets were delivered except for those people who had been absent. (Absence on pay day was a pretty good indicator that the ailment had been genuine.) I was finally

Offcuts 3

Peter Darmody

deposited back at my office and had to walk to the GPO to return the pistol and the unpaid wages.

Now, at that time, tight trousers with almost horizontal pockets that were cut across the abdomen were fashionable. As I walked along Queen Street I noticed a couple of girls ignoring my handsome face and giving their attention to the region considerably further south, smiling and nudging each other as they did so. I looked down to check the reason for their mirth. *Oh no!* 'Is that a gun in your pocket or are you just glad to see me?' I had no choice. I had to continue to my destination as nonchalantly as possible. The firearm safety instructions hadn't covered that contingency.

Suffice it to say that I never again wore those trousers on escort duty.

JEFF THORPE

DISASTER ON THE DERWENT

HOBART'S TASMAN BRIDGE spans the Derwent River,
for eastern shore residents the bridge does deliver
a three-minute drive to the city's heart,
as such, a vital link in no small part.

A high-arched viaduct, prestressed concrete girder design,
the bridge an impressive structure, certainly not benign,
supported by 21 pylons, o'er water thirty-five hundred feet,
by any assessable standards, a mountain of concrete.

January five 1975 became etched in Hobart's history,
a night of cold hard fact with not a trace of mystery,
when *Lake Illawarra* collided with the bridge,
this no slight nibble by a pesky midge.

Loaded with ten thousand tonnes of zinc concentrate,
Lake Illawarra was indeed no featherweight,
the bridge about three miles from its destination,
so near, yet so far in this misplaced navigation.

More Stories and Sketches from The Shed

The ship was off course and travelling too fast,
recipe for disaster which was bound not to last,
at 9:27 pm, the inevitable occurred,
the ship hit the bridge, unthinkable havoc incurred.

Two pylons and much roadway fell to the river and ship's deck,
four cars drove off the gap adding to the wreck,
five people in the cars were killed plus seven ship's crew,
the vessel quickly sank as the chaos grew.

*https://www.theguardian.com/australia-news/
2022/jan/05/a-picture-in-time-the-tasman-bridge-disaster*

On the bridge, two vehicles swayed on the brink of the gap,
their occupants very lucky to survive the flap,
being Sunday evening, bridge traffic was rather light
a certain saving grace for many from this blight.

An Inquiry found strong currents and Captain's inattention
the cause of the accident, a matter of contention,
a rumour at the time suggested Captain Belc was drunk
this unfounded though and the premise, like the ship, was sunk.

For careless navigation, Belc's sentence seemingly
    inadequate,
Master's Certificate six-month suspension inappropriate,
given the loss of lives and unrivalled damage brought about,
penalty somewhat paltry, carrying not much clout.

Yet, Captain Belc overall did not escape unscathed,
ship's owner Australian National Line had his ticket engraved
and retired the 60-year old, despite his stated intention,
to return to sea, post the forced abstention.

https://en.wikipedia.org/wiki/Tasman_Bridge_disaster

The loss of the bridge divided Hobart in two
thirty thousand living east side had to 'make do',
what had till then been a three-minute city commute
turned into a ninety-minute frustrating pursuit.

Offcuts 3

Services on the eastern shore were severely lacking
and soon, the social fabric of the locale was cracking,
in six months after the disaster crime rose 41 percent
while western side saw a crime rate descent.

Police figures also told a 50 percent rise in car theft,
a trebling of zone complaints showed a society bereft,
not surprising given the isolation easterners faced,
severance of the bridge left a bitter aftertaste.

Repair work on the bridge began in October 1975
yet 'twas almost three years before traffic on it could drive,
reconstruction added an extra traffic lane
and changes to shipping controls were put in train.

Vessels above a certain size need pilot navigation,
large ships passing 'neath the bridge need a tug in operation,
bridge traffic is suspended while big ships pass under,
designed to circumvent any seamanship blunder.

*https://commons.wikimedia.org/wiki/Category:
Tasman_Bridge_disaster#/media/File:Repair1976)
_(16014723680).jpg*

More Stories and Sketches from the Shed

Lake Illawarra and its cargo still lie thirty-four metres deep,
deemed no danger to shipping despite tidal sweep,
expert opinion believes the ship will not move
and to date no evidence found, this belief to disprove.

Hobart's risen from the ashes of January five '75,
the eastern shore has flourished and continues to thrive,
still, many have the memory, a deeply furrowed frown
of the tragedy that befell them, the night the bridge came down.

The Writers

As an Agricultural Scientist, **TREVOR ARMSTRONG** researched new non-crop weeds from developing countries. He organised the 1st John Armstrong's [who migrated from Lisboy, N. Ireland in 1852] descendants' gatherings at John's original *Spring Hill* restored homestead and compiled his family history book. Trevor and his wife Carol have enjoyed travelling to *Gathering of the Armstrong Clan* in Scotland, and through ten European plus African and Middle Eastern countries as well as around Australia via their A-Liner van. He voluntarily serves on Oxley Creek Catchment Association (OCCA) Management Committee and is currently its CreekCare Coordinator of thirteen weekly-visited BushCare sites, including Leader of Pennywort Creek BushCarers Habitat Brisbane Group.

WILLIAM (BILL) BARKER, the third eldest of nine brothers and one sister, grew up in Brisbane. He was conscripted for compulsory National Service in 1966, eventually serving from May 1968 for two years, in the Royal Australian Army Service Corps. William was stationed at Nui Dat, Vietnam, from May 1969 to May 1970. After National Service, with an economics degree, he entered primary school teaching and principalship. He married Mary in 1973. They have a daughter and three sons, thirteen grandchildren and two great grandsons. On retirement, he commenced wood-turning and took up traditional rocking horse carving. His stories are for his children and grandchildren.

JOHN BROWN was raised in the Great Depression and left school at age fourteen. He has an agricultural background, working sheep and cattle properties in Victoria, New South Wales and dairy farming in Queensland. He has three children, seven grandchildren and ten great grandchildren. He reached senior level by correspondence and became a Stock and Meat Inspector. John retired as Senior Inspector in charge of slaughterhouses, pet food and butchers' shops in 1987, and continued to play an active role in the church and community. In recent years he has enjoyed writing and publishing stories about his life and family.

DARRYL DYMOCK is Convenor of the motley mob known as the Writers Group at Oxley Men's Shed. He's also a published author and a mentor with the Queensland Writers Centre. As well as being a high school teacher, conscripted National Serviceman and (briefly) a taxi driver, for much of his professional life Darryl was a university teacher, and he has an honorary position at Griffith University. Early in 2024 he spent a month in Nepal with Australian Volunteers. He continues to write stories and take photos of the people and world around him, and he and his wife Cheryl enjoy their interactions with their four children and their families.

DAVID HANDS was born in Port Melbourne and completed an engineering degree at the University of Melbourne, followed by a Certificate at RMIT. He began working as an engineer in the construction industry on Melbourne Airport, and later moved to Alice Springs where he worked on the new hospital and a range of projects throughout the NT. He met his wife Yvonne there, and they have three children and seven grandchildren. From the NT they spent 10 years in Canberra, before moving to Brisbane where David joined a Consulting Engineering practice. David has worked on many projects throughout Australia and overseas, including the new Parliament House, Royal Brisbane Hospital, Hong Kong Airport and the Canberra Hospital.

OFFCUTS 3

JIM PASCOE has spent over sixty years in the Corinda and Oxley area. His entire career was spent in the electrical distribution network, starting his apprenticeship with the Brisbane City Council, Electricity Department, which became SEQEB, then Energex. He had a varied career in many departments before retiring as Technical Support Officer at the Call Centre. He was a member of the Royal Australian Navy Reserve until he married. He met his wife Janice in Warwick, where he spent the majority of his weekends. They have four children and thirteen grandchildren. He has been a member of the Oxley Men's Shed since its inception.

DAVE SHEARER's life started as a country boy in 1945 in South Australia, with five older siblings. At age 16 he joined the Army as an apprentice fitter and turner, then moved on to Army Aviation, training in aircraft maintenance in Queensland, and 15 months operational service in Vietnam. Dave married in 1970, and he and his wife have four children and six grandchildren. Following his discharge in 1971, he worked in Adelaide for Australia Post, then in South Australia and Queensland with the Federal Government Lighthouse Service as a mechanic. When the Service was privatised, he obtained a gas fitting licence and worked in this area until his retirement.

Initially trained as a plumber, the late **BILL THIRKILL** (1941–2024) was an active member of the Writers Group at the Shed from its inception in 2021 until near his untimely end. In that period he wrote more than 50 stories about his amazing life. At their fortnightly meetings, the other writers would sit in awe and sometimes disbelief as Bill told them about his adventures as a scuba diver, international skydiver, soldier, and especially as a tour manager, driving buses as a young man across 54 countries—in Asia and Europe, and later in Africa. He met his wife Fran on one of those early tours—they were engaged in Israel, married in England, then moved to New Zealand and finally to Australia, where they raised three children. Three of Bill's stories are included in this collection as a tribute to his significant contribution to the output of the Writers Group and in gratitude for the many memories he left with us.

Bush Poetry has been **JEFFREY THORPE**'s writing forté since 2008, after seeing a poet perform at Winton. Since then he has written some 300 poems and, as an Australian Bush Poets Association member, has had much of his work posted on the Association's website. These submissions have received thousands of viewings. He writes on a variety of subjects— historical events, things he sees around him, and episodes which have occurred in his life. For Jeff, writing is an enjoyable pastime and a challenge to 'bring to life' little known incidents.

OFFCUTS 3

GRAHAM TRIMBLE was born in rural Victoria, and his first 19 years were filled with hard physical farm work and looking after his five youngest siblings, from age 12. His mother was away from home for weeks at a time after their father died in 1955, and never married again. The two most important 'breaks' that changed Graham's life for the next 60+ years were: leaving home at age 16 to attend full-time Dookie Agricultural College, and courting and marrying Jan McNally. After graduating from Dookie, he taught for a total of 26+ years as a High School, TAFE and VET teacher, in both Queensland and Victoria, interspersed with 19+ years as an Insurance Agent/ Broker and Licensed Financial Planner.

JAMES VERNON had a variety of interests and occupations before his retirement. He trained to be a French horn player; had his own photographic studio; studied to be a high school teacher, and finally became a teacher of English to speakers of other languages and examiner for the International English Language Testing System. These occupations were interspersed with two periods of boredom in the Public Service. Now he is retired and spends his days reading, writing and pursuing his interest since he was ten years old in photography. Life is good.

The Artists

PETER DARMODY grew up on a sheep farm in the Monaro district of southern New South Wales. He studied in Sydney to become a high school teacher, but in 1967 he was called up for National Service and was posted to Papua New Guinea as an army education instructor. After National Service he worked initially as a teacher and then as an economist, mainly in Canberra. He has been drawing and painting for over 20 years and enjoys sketching on holidays and around Brisbane. Examples of Peter's work can be found on Instagram @petedarmody_art.

Despite the early disappointment of not winning a competition for his shark painting when he was four years old, **ANTHONY DURRINGTON** continued his artistic pursuits. A potter since 1988, he has also tried his hand at drawing, photography, graphic design and sculpture, even briefly dipping his toe into the world of glass-blowing and blacksmithing. The earth has turned full circle and after an almost 50-year hiatus he has returned to painting. He is looking forward to seeing where this leads him.

Offcuts 3

BRIAN GOELDNER was born in Brisbane in 1949, the eldest of four children. He is married with two daughters and four grandchildren. For 46 years he worked as a baker/pastrycook, owning the Market Cake Shop in Rocklea for 10 years, then Dominiques in Ipswich City Square. After retiring in 2012, Brian and his wife travelled extensively overseas. Since joining Oxley Men's Shed, he has very much enjoyed the camaraderie there, and through the drawing group has found a new outlet for his creativity.

Back in 1963 **GRAHAM MURPHY** attended an art class in the suburb of Woolloongabba on Saturday mornings, where he painted a lot of watercolour landscapes of outback Australia. He then continued art at school. A few years ago Graham painted a couple of Australian landscapes for friends living in London and Dublin, and recently has made a few pottery pieces. Graham is retired and lives in Sherwood with his wife, Kaye, and daughter, Sarah. His father-in-law, Harrold Whitting, who passed recently, inspired him to keep up painting, as he was a great artist. Joining the Oxley Men's Shed and discovering an Art Group there has enabled Graham to continue with his love of art.

GEORGE PUGH lives with his wife Lorraine in Inala, Brisbane. They have two children, six grandchildren and one great grandchild. George retired in 2000 after 36 years in the Queensland Police Service. He was a third-generation police officer, having followed in the footsteps of his father and his grandfather. During his police service, George was awarded the Queen's Commendation for Brave Conduct for his actions during the recapture of an escaped prisoner. After retirement George has been enjoying caravanning trips with his wife and attending the Oxley Men's Shed. He says that joining the Shed was the best decision he ever made.

With his wife and two sons, **PAUL WATKINS** migrated to Australia from Zimbabwe in 1989, settling in Toowoomba. He and Jean lived there for over 30 years before retiring to Corinda to be closer to the family. Apart from some brief lessons in sketching (as part of a TAFE drafting course) Paul has had no training in drawing. After seeing his granddaughter's skill at sketching, he decided to take advantage of the opportunity provided by the art group at the Shed, and is grateful for all the encouragement, camaraderie and fun he has experienced.

www.ingramcontent.com/pod-product-compliance
Lightning Source LLC
Chambersburg PA
CBHW050419120526
44590CB00015B/2029